Gukesh Dommaraju

Swayam Ganguly was born and raised in Jamshedpur and currently lives in Kolkata. He wears many hats: a published author, director of corporate films, editorial consultant for various publishers and a diehard aficionado of sports.

His interest in chess was cultivated at an early age, thanks to the sport being a regular feature among family and peers. After a gap of many years, Gukesh Dommaraju's remarkable achievement in the FIDE World Chess Championship 2024 drew Swayam to chess once again and inspired him to write a book.

qc Biographies

GUKESH DOMMARAJU

Swayam Ganguly

hachette INDIA

First published in 2025 by Hachette India
(Registered name: Hachette Book Publishing India Pvt.Ltd)
An Hachette UK company
www.hachetteindia.com

All chapters have been researched and written by Swayam Ganguly.

ISBN 978-93-5731-644-6

Hachette Book Publishing India Pvt. Ltd
4th/5th Floors, Corporate Centre,
Plot No. 94, Sector 44, Gurugram 122003, India

Typeset in Cambria 10.5/13 by Avishek Bhattacharya

MIX
Paper | Supporting responsible forestry
FSC® C010615

Printed and bound in India
by Thomson Press India Ltd.

Contents

Image Copyright Information		*vi*
Preface		*vii*
Chapter I:	History Created and Recreated	1
Chapter 2:	Gukesh's Journey to the Top of the World	11
Chapter 3:	The Chinese Blunder in Singapore	23
Chapter 4:	Two States	40
Chapter 5:	Gukesh and Magnus Carlsen – the Battle for Chess Supremacy	49
Chapter 6:	The Predictions: Before and After	61
Chapter 7:	The Humility and Simplicity of a Champion	72
Chapter 8:	The Training Regimen	82
Chapter 9:	Mental Toughness	92
Chapter 10:	The Hunger to Win	106
Chapter 11:	The Undisputed Leader of the New Generation	115
Chapter 12:	The Fans of the Prodigy	132
Chapter 13:	A Global Brand Ambassador?	143
Chapter 14:	The World Is My Family and the Family Is My World	159
Chapter 15:	The Alma Mater	166

Image Copyright Information

Page 3: Chessboard: Petey21/PD

Page 8: Vishwanath Anand: Wolfgang Jekel/CCA 2.0 Generic

Page 10: Gukesh with Richard Rapport: Vysotsky/CCA-SA 4.0 International licence

Page 22: Chess at Spanish court: Photographer not known, artist Luigi Mussini/ PD

Page 25: Gukesh versus Ding: Vysotsky/CCA-SA International licence

Page 39: Karpov in 1974: Copyright 2007, S.M.S.I., Inc. - Owen Williams, The Kasparov Agency/CCA-SA 3.0 Unported Licence

Karpov in 2015: Fryta 73 from Strzegom/CCA-SA 2.0 Generic

Page 43: Chaturanga: Chaturaji/CCA-SA 4.0 International Licence

Page 47: Chennai Bookfair: SmShameer/Shutterstock

Page 56: Carlsen: Stefan64/CCA-SA 3.0

Page 60: Karpov: ddisq/Shutterstock

Page 80: Alexander Alekhine: George Grantham Bain Collection (Library of Congress)/PD-US

Page 88: Gukesh and Arjun: Frans Peeters Photography/CCA-SA 2.0 generic licence

Page 91: Chess pieces: Sabelskaya/ Shutterstock

Page 95: Gukesh in 2023: Frans Peeters/CCA-SA 2.0 Generic

Gukesh in 2024: Eldar Azimov / Wikimedia Commons

Page 105: Gukesh vs Max Warmerdam: Vysotsky/CCA-SA 4.0 International licence

Page 113: Frans Peeters/CCA-SA 2.0 Generic

Page 114: Frans Peeters from Roosendaal, The Netherlands/ CCA-SA 2.0 Generic licence

Page 121: Vlad Ra27/Shutterstock

Page 124: Mikhail Tal: Ron Kroon for Anefo/CCA-SA 1.0 Universal Public Domain Dedication

Page 126: Mikhail Botvinnik: Harry Pot for Anefo/ CCA-SA 3.0 Netherlands Licence

Page 128: José Raúl Capablanca: Unknown (Keystone-France)/PD

Page 129: Bobby Fischer: Bert Verhoeff for Anefo/CC0 1.0 Universal Public Domain Dedication

Page 131: knight: Sore08 /Freepik

Page 133: Eldar Azimov / Wikimedia Commons/ CCA-SA 4.0 international licence

Page 142: Gukesh in 2023, at the Netherlands: Frans Peeters from Roosendaal, The Netherlands/CCA-SA 2.0 Generic licence

Page 143: Playing chess_generic: pedro7merino/Shutterstock

Page 150: Ding Liren: Mircea Moira/ Shutterstock

Page 153: Young Gukesh: GFHund/ CCA-SA 4.0 International licence

Page: 156: Shatranj: http://www.unesco.org/webworld/disclaimer.html

Page 161: Gukesh engrossed: Stefan64/CCA-SA 3.0 Unported licence

Page 163: Alireza Firouzja and Gukesh: Eldar Azimov / Wikimedia Commons/CCA-SA 4.0 international licence

Page 165: Gukesh with coat: Eldar Azimov / Wikimedia Commons/CCA-SA 4.0 International licence

Page 166: Velammal School: Bhadani at the English-language Wikipedia/ CCA-SA 3.0 Unreported licence

Page 182: Gukesh with president: PIB

Icons: queen: SN VFX/Shutterstock; chess piece in white background: Pixel-Shot/Shutterstock; knight: creatorz vision/Freepik; bullet icon: rawpixel.com/Freepik; 6 chess pieces icon: creatorz vision/Freepik

Preface

In late 2024 Gukesh Dommaraju burst upon the international scene becoming the youngest-ever world chess champion. While well known in chess circles, this win made him a household name in India, and brought him into the limelight.

Not too much is known about him and this book aims to fill that void to a certain extent. Even now, the absolute detailing needed will take years to emerge, possibly with an official biography or autobiography. But he has been a promising Indian chess star exhibiting clear signs of extraordinary talent, perseverance and stamina. His dedication, calmness and modesty are lessons for all. While we read about his achievements, we also look at the areas he needs to improve. He remains unperturbed, learns from mistakes and never shies at further challenges.

Gukesh knows how to rise to the top with hard work and unwavering focus. But more importantly, the eighteen-year-old has already mastered the art of not being swayed by momentous success and all the overblown criticism that success strings along with it. To top it all, he always remembers, 'My mother urges me to be a good human being above anything else.'

This well-researched saga of success talks about Gukesh's childhood, friends and family and outlines the build-up to the World Chess Championship 2024, in Singapore, where he emerged as the youngest ever world champion. The inspirational narrative highlights his mentors – his parents, coaches, teachers, peers, and other well-wishers whose ineffable significance in his journey so far can never be overstated.

The latest addition to Hachette's 'Quick and Concise Biographies' series, *Gukesh Dommaraju* also throws light on the journey of the Indian-origin cerebral pastime, called chess, across the world through a weft of modification and customization. The book introduces the early masters and legendary grandmasters who are the much needed context and legacy that resulted in Gukesh's win. For the uninitiated it also explains the ranking systems, basic and special chess rules, and iconic moves. Thus, with practical guidance on how to become a grandmaster, benefits of playing chess and so on, this simple and accessible biography doubles as a chess primer too.

This inviting gateway to the world of chess is loaded with statistics, memorable quotes and amazing facts; and on the whole will introduce the reader to a fascinating game and its world and now its newest star.

Dedicated to my elder brother, Rupam Ganguly,
a true chess aficionado.

I

HISTORY CREATED AND RECREATED

Every chess master was once a beginner.
– Irving Chernev
(Chess player and author)

The year was 2013. The World Chess Championship was being hosted in Chennai, and it was the talk of the town. Indian grandmaster Viswanathan Anand was locked in battle with Norwegian grandmaster Magnus Carlsen for the top honours in world chess. Among the audience that thronged the packed hall at the Hyatt Regency was a seven-year-old boy named Gukesh Dommaraju, who was a keen chess enthusiast. Gukesh had accompanied his father to the mega event. But all the seats were taken and this little boy had to stand at the back of the hall along with his father to witness this grand spectacle.

As Gukesh stared into the glass box where the two superstars of chess were engaged in a battle of wits and skill, he dreamed of being inside that same box one day. How cool would that be! But the following days would end in disappointment for all Indian chess fans, and especially the ones watching the live heated duel indoors between the two gladiators in the glass enclosure as the sweltering Chennai heat raged outside. Gukesh was heartbroken as Magnus Carlsen would go on to defeat his hero, Viswanathan Anand, to be crowned the new world champion. At that impressionable age, this defeat was painful for a young

Indian chess enthusiast like Gukesh who saw his idol Vishy Sir losing his crown. 'I shall bring back the title to India,' a young Gukesh pledged. This thought was gradually transformed into passion and then into an obsession. But eleven years later, this dream was actually converted into reality when the eighteen-year-old chess prodigy named Gukesh Dommaraju recreated history in Singapore by becoming the second Indian world chess champion and also made history by becoming the youngest world chess champion. He also became the third world chess champion from Asia. He had brought back the crown for India in his very first attempt, which was a stupendous achievement to say the least.

Chennai Airport was crowded with fans who had gathered to welcome their new world chess champion. Some of them had arrived as early as 7.30 a.m. to catch a glimpse of him. The fans who awaited Gukesh's arrival at the T2 international arrival gate of Chennai Airport were charged and ready to welcome their new hero, armed with colourful banners and flags. But by 10.30 a.m., the energy and excitement became a bit subdued as the fans started becoming restless and impatient because the flight had not landed yet. Where was Gukesh? When would their hero arrive? The media crew was crouched in their exclusive corners complete with still and video cameras and flash bulbs, ready to shoot some exclusive footage of the world champion. Officials from the Sports Development Authority of Tamil Nadu were in attendance and Gukesh's father Dr Rajinikanth had also arrived at the airport. Everyone awaited the national hero and the world chess champion with eager anticipation and their patience was duly rewarded when the chess prodigy's flight finally landed. It was definitely worth the wait for the fans, who erupted in joy when Gukesh stepped out of the airport, adorned with the Indian tricolour, wearing a king's crown on his head and a giant garland around his neck. But what drew the largest cheers was the glittering World Championship trophy that the young champion held in his hand. It had finally come home.

The Basics of **Chess**

Chess is a strategy game that is played by two players. These players take turns to make moves on the chessboard with the goal of capturing the king of the opponent. A chessboard has sixty-four squares with eight rows and eight columns, and these are known as 'ranks' or 'files' respectively. There are sixteen pieces assigned to each player, comprising eight pawns, two knights, two bishops, two rooks, one queen and one king. A player is assigned either a white or black set of pieces, and the player who is assigned the white pieces has the right to make the first move in the game of chess. Each of the players must take turns to make their move and the goal is not to put their king in check. Each of the pieces has their own unique way of moving across the chessboard. The pawns, for example, can only move forward unless they are capturing a piece of the opponent, in which case, they can move diagonally. The knights can move in 'L' shapes, and the movement either happens two squares vertically and one square horizontally or two squares horizontally and one square vertically. The knights also have the power to move by jumping over the other pieces as the game is taking place. The bishops can move diagonally backwards or forwards across the chessboard for any amount of spaces. The rooks can also move forwards or backwards either horizontally or vertically across the board for any number of spaces. The queen is the most powerful piece and can move in any direction vertically, diagonally or horizontally for any number of spaces. The king, however, can move just one square in any direction.

Just when it seemed that everything was going smoothly, chaos descended as everyone wanted to get up close and personal with the local hero. History repeated itself again in the form of frenzy of the fans after an international win by an Indian athlete or a World Cup triumph. The crowd was so determined to catch a glimpse of their chess champion that not even the police could control them. The local press added to the chaos, all of them eager to catch a soundbite or photograph or video bite that would make them heroes in their respective media houses. All the fans wanted selfies with Gukesh, and he graciously and patiently obliged everyone he could. But Dr Rajinikanth was unable to escort his son to the car waiting outside because of the sea of people surrounding them. Before matters worsened, Gukesh and his father were whisked away by a cordon of cops and officials and escorted home in a specially decorated car, which bore Gukesh's name and face along with his spectacular achievement: the new king in the Kingdom of Chess. There was also an inscription on the car that said: 18@18, which signified Gukesh Dommaraju becoming the eighteenth world chess champion at the age of eighteen.

This was an extraordinary feat as not only did Gukesh become the youngest-ever world chess champion but also defeated the reigning champion, Ding Liren of China, thus cementing his position among the best players in chess across the world. The thrilling contest of the 2024 World Chess Championship raged on for fourteen games. Gukesh was clearly experiencing a battle of nerves apart from the battle against his formidable opponent. The moment that he had dreamed of as a young boy was finally before him. Ding Liren had won the first game and it seemed that the Chinese was sailing away to defend his title successfully when the unthinkable happened. Gukesh made a great comeback by calming his nerves and clinching game 3 and drawing level. In life, we are all provided with that one opportunity that we must grab in order to become extraordinary from ordinary. That moment is ours to seize and we must do so or wait for that moment to arrive again. Lady Luck smiles at us during that moment and it's gone in a flash. This moment might never arrive again if we fail to act upon it and take advantage of the stars. The next seven games between Gukesh and Ding Liren saw seven draws and now Gukesh was just one match away from realizing his dream for India. That's when the Chinese grandmaster made a silly mistake with his rook that cost him the game. This was that defining moment in Gukesh's eighteen-year-old life. He pounced on the opportunity created by the blunder to drive home the advantage and take the game, the match as well as the title of world champion.

Probably the most impressive part about this victory was the tremendous tactical brilliance, maturity and chess skills displayed by this new world champion at such a young age. Gukesh admitted later that he did not expect to win that crucial final game as it appeared to be heading towards a draw. In fact, he was playing for a draw before that cloud with a silver lining presented itself when his Chinese opponent made that silly mistake. To be fair, Ding Liren played a good game. But Gukesh maintained his calmness and composure throughout the match, winning just one more game than the Chinese grandmaster. When asked later about the match and the high-pressure situation involved during the face-off with Ding Liren, Gukesh admitted that he was really stressed out during this crucial encounter.

'I wasn't feeling very enthusiastic,' Gukesh confessed later. This was an indication that his nerves were greatly affected when the game began. 'I went through a lot of emotions during this match. I lost the first game. I had so many emotions to go through. I was a bit stressful and got caught up with the pressure of the moment. And at that moment what really helped was those close to me reminded me why I fell in love with the sport in the first place.'

The teenager displayed his mettle, drive, fighting spirit and resilience as he came from behind and pounced on a single error from his vastly experienced Chinese opponent to win the title. He also demonstrated the grit and determination that had kept him going through all the hurdles and obstacles to reach his goal single-mindedly. This was the goal he had pursued since he had watched his hero relinquish the crown to another emerging champion. Today, it was his day. He had made everyone proud, including his idol and mentor, Viswanathan Anand. When Gukesh had first laid eyes on the chessboard and the chess pieces that came with it, he was seven years old. That's when he had started playing chess. Some diehard fanatics might argue that he was a late starter compared to other prodigies and champions like Grandmasters Sergey Karjakin and Magnus Carlsen, who had both picked up the game when they were just five years old. But then none of them were the youngest chess champion in the world, were they?. When Gukesh started playing chess, the chessboard was just a toy for him and he had no clue what being a world champion meant. Over the years, it blossomed into a more intense passion as he breathed and lived chess. The only constant is that deep down he thinks he is still that kid who fell in love with chess. That kid had just checkmated history and recreated it on his own terms.

As India celebrated its new world champion in chess, Gukesh celebrated in his own characteristic style after winning the crown by restacking his chess pieces, breaking into sobs, shutting his pen and posing like Roger Federer after a Grand Slam victory. However, it is Novak Djokovic that he idolizes as a tennis player, and this is hardly surprising as both Gukesh and his tennis idol have similar playing styles and sporting temperaments even though they practise different sports. Closer observation has revealed that both players are not heavily reliant on opening preparation before their games. Both play the game according to their wishes or as they see fit, innovating and devising strategies according to the demands of the game and during its natural progression. Both Djokovic and Gukesh are completely original and creative players in their respective sports. But while Djokovic has been nicknamed 'the Joker' for his on-field antics, Gukesh is calmness and composure personified and a rare blend of humility and talent. Gukesh's chess idol, five-time world champion Viswanathan Anand, said: 'Gukesh became the eighteenth world champion in the sport in what will have a massive impact on chess in India. Gukesh is the third world champion from Asia, the second one from India. The second one from Tamil Nadu and Chennai as well. That's one nice thing. I think at a global level, what will stand out is that he is the youngest world champion in history, beating the previous record by three years. Eighteen is just an unbelievable age to become world champion.'

The Lightning Kid

Viswanathan Anand is the one who popularized the advancement of chess in India. He is the one who kindled the fire, which was always burning. But every fire needs that spark to ignite it, and he was that rare spark. The five-time world chess champion became a household name in India. Here are some amazing facts about the best rapid chess player of his generation, who received the nickname 'Lightning Kid'.

- Born on 11 December 1969, in Mayiladuthurai, Tamil Nadu, Anand inherited his love for chess from his mother Sushila, who was a chess player. She started mentoring Anand when he was six years old. Thank God for mothers!

- He was the youngest Indian to become an international master and was also India's first grandmaster.

- Viswanathan Anand is also called 'Vishy' and 'Tiger of Madras' because of his dominant exploits in the world of chess. In 2000, Anand became the first Indian to become the world chess champion after defeating Alexei Shirov. From 2007 to 2013, he dominated the world of chess by winning the World Chess Championship five times. He received the Chess Oscar, the international award given to the best chess player every year, as many as six times.

- Viswanathan Anand was awarded the prestigious Padma Shri Award when he was only eighteen years old. He was the first Indian sports star to receive the Padma Vibhushan Award in 2008. He was also the first sportsperson to receive the Rajiv Gandhi Khel Ratna Award, which is India's highest sporting honour.

- The Lightning Kid has a flair for languages as well. He is fluent in Tamil, English, French, German and Spanish. His book *Vishy Anand: My Best Games of Chess* is a must-read for all chess lovers as it encapsulates his incredible journey.

No wonder Viswanathan Anand received the British Chess Federation 'Book of the Year' Award for this book in 1998.

- Even the stars or the sky is not the limit for the great Viswanathan Anand as an entire planet was needed to pay tribute to him. In 1988, a minor planet that was discovered was named after this legend. The planet has been officially named '(4538) Vishyanand'.

Gukesh versus Richard Rapport in the Netherlands in 2023

2

GUKESH'S JOURNEY TO THE TOP OF THE WORLD

Chess is not for timid souls.
– Wilhelm Steinitz
(First world chess champion, 1886–94)

Gukesh Dommaraju's extraordinary milestone to become the youngest world chess champion in 2024 followed his triumph at the Candidates Tournament. Here, Gukesh was the youngest player ever to qualify for a World Chess Championship match. So the victory over Ding Liren was more of a well-planned career progression rather than just a shock victory as perceived by some international experts. This becomes evident when one considers the fact that Gukesh is the third-youngest grandmaster in the history of chess. From India, only Viswanathan Anand has managed to win the prestigious Candidates Tournament before Gukesh, who became the second Indian to do so and qualify for a World Chess Championship. Gukesh is also the youngest chess player to go past an Elo rating of 2700. Not only did he reach an Elo rating of 2750, but he also smashed several records on the way. Someone famously said, 'Life is a journey, not a destination.'

The journey of Gukesh in the kingdom of chess might have just begun, but the road traversed has been exciting and the road that curves ahead promises to herald a golden era in Indian chess.

What is the Elo Rating System?

The Elo rating system is a method used to calculate the relative skills of players in games like chess or e-sports. It was invented to improve the chess-rating system, making the previous Harkness system redundant and is named after its creator, Hungarian-American physics professor Arpad Elo. The Elo rating system was so effective that it has been successfully employed in other sports like football, baseball, basketball, American football, pool, e-sports and several board games. In recent years, large-language models (LLM) have also used it as an effective rating system. The outcome of a match is predicted by using the difference in the ratings between the two players in this system. If two players have equal ratings and face each other, the outcome is expected to be an equal number of wins. The player who is rated 100 points more than his opponent, for example, is expected to score 64 per cent in the match or have a win percentage of 64. With a rating difference of 200 points, this percentage escalates to 76 per cent according to the Elo rating system. A player's Elo ratings keep changing after every game or tournament in chess, and the winning player takes points from the losing player after each game to add to his tally of points. However, if a higher-rated player wins a match, only a few points will be deducted from the tally of the lower-ranked losing player. But in case of an upset by a lower-ranked player, he will get more points after beating a higher-rated player or drawing with him. The Elo ratings are reflective of a comparative analysis and do not reflect the strength or the capability of an individual player. A complete novice in chess might have a rating of 1000 Elo while the ratings for the best chess players in history might range from 2800 Elo and above.

The Elo Rating System – Range and Category	
Rating range	**Category**
2700+	Informal title of 'Super Grandmasters'
2700–2500	Grandmasters (GM)
2499–2400	International Masters (IM)
2399–2300	FIDE Masters (FM)

Gukesh Dommaraju was born on 29 May 2006 in Chennai, Tamil Nadu, to Dr Rajinikanth and Dr Padmakumari. Gukesh's mother is a microbiologist and his father is an ENT (ear, nose and throat) surgeon. It was expected that the son would follow in the footsteps of his parents and show interest in medicine as a career. But that was not to be as Gukesh was hooked to chess like a fish to water from an early age. This keen interest was first observed by his school coach, Mr Bhaskar, who taught Gukesh the basics of the game. He was seven years old when he began playing chess, attending three classes every week. He was a quick learner and began training under the watchful eyes of his first coach. His coach noticed Gukesh's skill and potential and encouraged him to participate in weekend tournaments in the city. In a span of just six months, Gukesh's first FIDE rating was an impressive 1291.

> A standard FIDE chess rating begins only at 1000 Elo and great, experienced chess players normally have a rating between 1500 and 2000.

It helped the cause that Gukesh attended the Velammal Vidyalaya School in Mel Ayanambakkam, Chennai. This school has branches across the city of Chennai and is famous for producing young chess talents who went on to become grandmasters like Karthikeyan Murali, Aravindh Chithambaram and R. Praggnanandhaa. The school was especially supportive of Gukesh's chess career, permitting him to skip classes and only attend school during his examinations. Everyone noticed the natural talent in him and wanted him to focus only on chess without any distractions. Gukesh was playing weeklong rating tournaments within a year's time. Thankfully, his parents realized that their son was a chess prodigy and supported him fully so that he could realize his dream of being a full-time chess player. His parents also had to make sacrifices so that their son realized his chess dreams. His mother increased her duties as a microbiologist by assuming additional responsibilities in increased work shifts. His father became a part-time doctor to be able to travel with his son during his tournaments outside Chennai. Later, Gukesh's father quit his medical career to manage his son's career. Today everything is managed by his father, including Gukesh's travel plans, invitations and social media handles. It is because of this support that Gukesh has reached the pinnacle of success. Having mere talent is not enough as it has to be nurtured and shaped so that a blooming flower can be transformed in due course into a beautiful fruit-bearing tree.

In 2015, Gukesh won the Asian School Chess Championships in the under-9 section to receive the status of Candidate Master. In 2017, he fulfilled all the requirements needed for the title International Chess Master at 34th Cappelle-la-Grande Open. This transition to the rank of international master (IM) was quick by anyone's standards as he managed to achieve the mandatory three IM norms in only six months. Norms in chess mean certain performance standards that a player must reach in particular tournaments that are FIDE-approved. Gukesh scored 7 out of the maximum 9 points at the Cappelle-la-Grande Open to secure his final norm and become an IM in March 2018. The very next month, he participated in the Asian Youth Chess Championship where he secured five golds thanks to his wins in the categories of under-12 individual rapid chess, under-12 individual blitz, under-12 classical chess, under-12 blitz team and the under-12 rapid team event. The next goal that Gukesh had set himself was to become a GM, or grandmaster, which was the highest officially recognized title in the sport of chess. In April 2018, he participated at the Bangkok Open to achieve his first GM norm. The second GM norm was secured in Serbia in December of the same year. All that was left now was the final norm in his quest to become GM. The opportunity presented itself quickly in December 2018 at the Sunway Sitges International Chess Festival. This was a huge moment because if Gukesh succeeded in achieving his final norm, he would become the youngest grandmaster in the history of chess. But alas! Greatness must be hard fought to achieve. Gukesh had to win his final game to achieve his final norm. He fell agonizingly short as the game ended in a draw. Although this was a disappointment at the time, Gukesh displayed his hunger and determination even at that young age. The wait for his quest wasn't long, however, as it took him just one more month to become a grandmaster. On the historic day of 15 January 2019, Gukesh achieved his third and final GM norm at the Delhi

International Grandmaster Open. He was aged twelve years, seven months and seventeen days, narrowly missing the record for the youngest chess grandmaster, which was held by Russian grandmaster Sergey Karjakin, who had become a grandmaster at the age of twelve years and seven months. The difference was only seventeen days! Indian chess fans will derive comfort from the fact that it was a chess player of Indian origin who eventually broke the record for the youngest grandmaster. This happened when Indian-origin American chess player Abhimanyu Mishra achieved the feat in 2021, aged twelve years, four months and twenty-five days.

Gukesh was simply relentless in his pursuit of the title of grandmaster as he played a mind-boggling 276 games in as many as thirty tournaments in a span of only sixteen months between the periods of winning his first IM norm to his final GM norm. After becoming a grandmaster, Gukesh's performance was enhanced to another level. In February 2020, he emerged as the winner of a tournament organized by the Hillerød Chess Club in Denmark. In 2022, his home city hosted the FIDE Chess Olympiad. Gukesh was placed in the team India 2, which he helped reach third place in the tournament. He also won the gold medal on board one, on which the top-ranked players competed in a round-robin format. In the eleven games he played, Gukesh won eight games. In October 2022, he faced reigning world champion Magnus Carlsen in the Aimchess Rapid online tournament. He beat Carlsen in this match, and it was considered a major upset in chess circles as he was the youngest player to defeat Magnus Carlsen in an official chess game after the Norwegian grandmaster became the world champion. It was clear that Gukesh was knocking on the door that led to the top position in chess. Magnus Carlsen got his revenge in the FIDE Chess World Cup held in August 2023 when he beat Gukesh in the quarterfinals of the tournament. The updated FIDE ratings were released on September 2023 and Viswanathan Anand was dethroned from his position as the highest-ranked Indian chess player. India's first grandmaster and former world champion had held this position for as long as thirty-seven years. But there was a new kid on the block who had beaten him this time. His name was Dommaraju – Gukesh Dommaraju.

Cut to the 2024 chess olympiad hosted by Budapest, Hungary where India won its first gold with Gukesh's help. He picked up the gold medal again on board one, winning eight games and drawing two in his total of ten games. Even the Indian women's team won the gold at this tournament, making it a double bonanza. It was a proud and historic day for Indian chess. The 2024 Candidates Tournament was an important event for Gukesh as it would decide which player would challenge the reigning world champion Ding Liren. But Gukesh had to first qualify for the Candidates Tournament, which he did in December 2023. He had finished in second place behind Fabiano Caruana in the 2023 FIDE Circuit. However, Caruana had already qualified for the Candidates Tournament by finishing third in the 2023 FIDE Chess World Cup. That meant that the empty slot went to Gukesh and this was a stroke of luck when it was needed the most. He was perceived an underdog at the 2024 Candidates Tournament which comprised eight top international chess players including Ian Nepomniachtchi, Hikaru Nakamura, Nijat Abasov and Alireza Firouzja, along with the Indians Rameshbabu Praggnanandhaa and Vidit Gujrathi. But Gukesh surprised the experts and critics alike with his superlative performance at the Candidates. He made a comeback after a loss against the more fancied Alireza Firouzja to beat him in five games straight to earn a half-point lead before the final round.

All Gukesh needed now was a win in his final round against Hikaru Nakamura to win the championship. If Gukesh drew against Nakamura, that would have led to a playoff in case Nepomniachtchi or Caruana won their last game, where they were playing each other. But both the matches between Gukesh and Nakamura as well as Nepomniachtchi and Caruana ended in draws. Lady Luck smiled on Gukesh again and he was adjudged the winner. The underdog had become the top dog. Gukesh became the youngest player in chess history to win the Candidates Tournament aged seventeen years, ten months and twenty-four days. He broke the record of chess legend Garry Kasparov, who had previously won the title in 1983–84 as a twenty-one-year-old. This record had stood for almost forty years.

When Gukesh faced Ding in the 2024 FIDE World Chess Championship in Singapore from 25 November to 13 December 2024, he was rated higher than Ding before the event began despite being the challenger. So even though Gukesh wasn't fancied to win by the pundits, he could in no way be termed as the underdog in this fight. The world championship involved fourteen games and the first player to reach 7.5 points would be declared the winner and the champion of the world. In the event that both players would be tied at 7 points each after the fourteen games, rapid games would come into play. Gukesh started with White but lost the first match to Ding. Gukesh won Game 3 to level the scores. Then a series of draws followed before Gukesh surged into the lead after winning game 11. But Ding levelled the score to 6–6 after twelve games were completed. The last game, game 14, began with Ding on White and was headed for a draw before Ding made an absolute blunder on the fifty-fifth move. Gukesh leapt to take the advantage instantly and a shocked and dejected Ding resigned. The rest, as they say, is history.

A Brief History of **Chess**

- It's widely believed that the game of chess originated in India. Before the sixth century CE, it was called chaturanga and later came to be known as shatranj. Chess was then picked up in Persia by the Arabs. In fact, it was the Arabs who are credited for coining the term 'Shah Mat', which means 'the king is dead'. It is this word that gave rise to the term 'checkmate' in chess. Evidence of chess spreading quickly and far and wide was found when archaeologists unearthed ivory playing pieces and chess artefacts in Uzbekistan that date back as early as year 760. Chess reached Europe much later, sometime in the year 1000. It took a long time for it to evolve and reach its present form as considerable changes were made to the game sometime around 1475, when formal rules were added. The first standard chess manual came out in 1749 to make things more formal. Chess master François-André Danican Philidor wrote this manual named *Analyse du jeu des Échecs*. It covered some new opening ideas and the defence, which still bears his name. The book or manual also featured Philidor's famous defence in rook and pawn endgames. This endgame technique is still in use. A famous statement in this book was

'The pawns are the soul of chess'. But it was only during the period between the eighteenth century and the 1880s that chess received its major makeover and assumed its present structure. Until then chess had moved at a snail's pace. The three important laws of chess that were put into motion were stalemate rules, the use of pawns as strategic pieces and the convention of white pieces having the first right of movement. No wonder this period is known as the Romantic Era of chess.

- Before the game of chess reached Europe, it passed through the Islamic world from India. Earlier, chess pieces in the Indian version resembled actual soldiers, bishops and kings. But due to religious reasons, the chess pieces were built in the manner they are today. Even after chess spread to a predominantly Christian Europe, the chess pieces remained much the same.

- The second book that was ever printed in the English language was about chess.

- The oldest recorded chess game in history is from the 900s, and this game was played between a historian from Baghdad and his student.

- A Spanish priest named Ruy Lopez is considered to be one of the first known masters of the game of chess. There is an opening named after him, although he did not invent it. But he did analyse it in his book that he published in 1561, much before Philidor's famous chess manual of course. However, some of the chess theory advocated by Lopez wouldn't be advisable under any circumstances in today's world. He actually suggested the strategy of playing chess with the sun in the eyes of the opponent.

♟ The modern version of chess prevalent today surfaced in the sixteenth century. Before that there were no clocks to mark the duration of play, and even the pieces were standardized only in the nineteenth century. In 1849, a manufacturer of games and toys named Jaques of London brought forth a new style of chess pieces designed by Nathaniel Cooke and known as the Staunton pattern. These became popular in chess playing circles and were used in all the clubs and tournaments across the world. Some minor variations have been made to the Staunton pieces, of course, but they have become the standard chess sets for every tournament globally to date. The nineteenth century also witnessed the advent of chess clocks to boost rapid competitive play. Before chess clocks, a chess game could go on for an excruciating fourteen hours. Thanks to this landmark invention, the final seal of approval was given in terms of equipment needed in a modern chess tournament. Chess had now reached precision and perfection. Naturally, the first official world championship was held in the late nineteenth century. In 1886, Wilhelm Steinitz became the first official world champion and held on to his title till 1894, when he was dethroned by Emanuel Lasker.

♟ After the first few big tournaments were successfully concluded, various modern styles of play began to develop and emerge. Even though the first book on chess openings was published in 1843, as mentioned earlier, the evolution of the theory of these openings only evolved during the early- and mid-twentieth century. The late twentieth century saw the introduction of databases and computer engines. With technology moving forward at a mind-boggling speed, the future of chess promises to be an exciting one.

A Chess Challenge at the Court of Spain (a famous painting that depicts a match held in 1575 in Madrid, Spain)

3

THE CHINESE BLUNDER IN SINGAPORE

Blunders rarely travel alone.
– Anatoly Karpov
(Former world chess champion from Russia)

It was 12 December 2024. There was a tense atmosphere in the room in Singapore where the World Chess Champion Ding Liren from China locked horns with the Indian challenger Gukesh Dommaraju. After a total of thirteen games played between the two players, the World Chess Championship was tied at 6.5 points each. The fourteenth game was the final game and extremely crucial as it would decide who would be the chess champion of the world. Both the players dug into their reserves of strategy, wits and mental toughness for this all-important game. But not even the wisest of experts could have predicted what would follow next. As the clock ticked down on the final game, it appeared that the game was headed for a tame draw.

Ding, who was renowned in chess circles for his calmness in pressure situations and particularly great skills when it came to endgame, made a crucial error in judgment. As they say, it isn't over till it's over. In sports, the margin of victory and defeat is very narrow and you can never take anything for granted. Ding focused on forcing a draw instead of trying to win the match for a simple reason – if the match went into a draw, the championship winner would be then decided in rapid tie-breaks. Ding was aware that he would have the advantage in such a scenario over his Indian challenger who was more suited to the classical form of playing chess, and rapid tie-breaks was not his forte. That is when Ding let down his guard and made a major mistake, which will probably haunt him for the rest of his life. This was a move so strange that it confused even the stoic Gukesh. Ding moved his rook from f4 to f2, and it was such a harmless move that it almost seemed routine. Gukesh studied the chessboard keenly as the move opened up a new possibility for him. 'But how could Ding make such an error?' he wondered. Was Ding setting a trap for him by making such a move? As Gukesh speedily considered all the possibilities of such a move, he was baffled as none of them appeared logical. There was only one explanation for Ding's move. The Chinese grandmaster had made a vital error in trying to force a draw and had handed Gukesh a marvellous opportunity on a platter to breach his defences. There was pin-drop silence in the room as Gukesh pondered over his next move before going in for the kill. This was simple execution. All he would have to do now was enforce a simple exchange of rooks that would be followed by an important move with his bishop. That would reduce Ding to an impossible situation. Ding realized the folly of his move now. Two of his opponent's pawns would now stride into his corner of the chessboard to be promoted into mightier warriors, rendering him helpless as Ding's single pawn stood immobile and his king was surrounded.

Ding's eyes widened in horror as the realization dawned upon him about the enormity of his blunder even before Gukesh's move. As Gukesh made his move just like Ding had known he would, a distraught Ding buried his head into his hands in apparent dejection. So close and yet so far! How could he have made such an error under pressure when he was known for his calmness in pressure situations? Gukesh broke into silent tears after winning the match. Devastated in defeat but never lacking sporting spirit, Ding Liren rose and shook hands with the young, new champion of the world.

However, the chess world wasn't united in celebrating the success of the Indian champion. The ugly face of controversy

Ding (left) and Gukesh (right) during the 2023 FIDE World Championship

revealed itself instantly. The first person to question the legitimacy of Gukesh's win was Andrei Filatov, the brash and outspoken president of the Russian Chess Federation. He alleged that there was foul play in the match almost immediately after the match without a congratulatory message for Gukesh. In an attacking social media post, Filatov accused Ding of throwing away the game – and this is a serious allegation for sure.

The Historic Victory

A Timeline

Here's a breakdown of the 14-game series that was held between the challenger Gukesh and the reigning world champion Ding Liren in Singapore for the title of world champion.

- Game 1: Ding Liren won the first game conclusively, to take a 1–0 lead after Gukesh struggled to find his rhythm and strategy. The game lasted just forty-two moves.

- Game 2: Gukesh bounced back into the competition in game 2, which however, ended in a draw. But Gukesh had 0.5 points now and Liren had 1.5 points.

- Game 3: Gukesh made a solid comeback in game 3 as he outplayed Ding Liren with his moves and strategies to win the first game of the series. The score now was 1.5–1.5.

- Game 4: Gukesh played confidently now, after his win in game 3 in this intense game, which ended in a draw. The scores were still level at 2 points each after four games.

- Game 5: Gukesh dominated game 5, but it ended in a draw as well, keeping the scores even at 2.5 points each.

- Game 6: This was an evenly matched contest as the Indian and Chinese grandmasters locked horns with each other. Another draw and scores still level at 3 points each.
- Game 7: This game was a marathon affair, lasting for five hours and twenty-two minutes as both players played cautiously and patiently. It was another draw now with the scores level at 3.5 points each. The halfway mark was reached and there was no sign of a clear winner yet.
- Game 8: The tension was evident on the faces as this game also ended in a draw. Both players were on 4 points each and even the audience was on the edge of their seats.
- Game 9: The suspense was kept alive after game 9, which was also a draw. Both players were now on 4.5 points.
- Game 10: It was the same story with game 10 tied as well. Both players were on 5 points, but the excitement of the audience had reached fever-pitch.
- Game 11: After so many ties, game 11 upped the contest and Gukesh won as he made the most of an error made by Liren on the twenty-eighth move. Gukesh led Liren now 6–5.
- Game 12: Gukesh played more confidently now, but Liren bounced back to win game 12 to equal

the score 6–6. The series was like a see-saw.

- Game 13: Liren applied pressure on Gukesh now in his attempt to regain his title, but Gukesh maintained his composure to fight back. Game 13 was eventually tied.

- Game 14: The final game was the decider. If game 14 was tied, it would go into tie-breakers. It appeared that the game was headed for a tie. Ding Liren obviously fancied his chances in the tie-breaker and he played for a draw now. But Gukesh was relentless in his search for a win even though the game looked like it was headed for a draw. It was then that Ding Liren succumbed to the pressure and made a silly mistake or blunder that cost him the game, the match and the championship. Gukesh moved in for the kill and won the final game and the crown, 7.5 to 6.5.

'The behaviour of the Chinese player during the decisive moments is highly suspicious and warrants a thorough investigation by FIDE,' Filatov raged. He termed the Chinese debacle in Singapore 'inexplicable,' and hinted that Ding's actions were unacceptable for a player of his stature.

Former world champion Vladimir Kramnik added fuel to the fire as he labelled the game of chess 'disappointingly weak' in its present form and called Ding's blunder 'childish'. Kramnik also questioned the quality of play in the World Chess Championship and stressed upon its deterioration in the present day and age. He went far enough to call it 'the end of chess as we know it'.

FIVE FAMOUS BLUNDERS IN CHESS

Blunders are probably the worst thing one can make. In chess, blunders can be catastrophic and lead to throwing away a winning advantage in a match.

1. Mikhail Chigorin

In 1886, Austrian-American grandmaster Wilhelm Steinitz became the first official World Champion in the history of chess and ruled as the top boss in chess till the late 1800s. In 1892, he was challenged by Russian grandmaster Mikhail Chigorin, who sought revenge after being defeated by Steinitz in the 1889 World Championship. The challenge was accepted and the match was scheduled to take place in Havana, Cuba. The two chess warriors remained even-steven till game 21, until Steinitz won game 22. In game 23, Chigorin had to draw or win to keep the match going. He had an advantage early on in the game and in his eagerness to win, the Russian made a big slip-up to lose the game.

The defending champion Wilhelm Steinitz was leading 9-8, and Mikhail Chigorin looked like levelling things as he was in a winning position in the next game. But he could not find his best move needed to win the match. Instead, Chigorin played 32 Bb4 to attack one of Black's rooks, which was a big mistake. Chigorin lost the advantage of all the hard work he had done thanks to this silly mistake.

2. Tigran Petrosian

The 1956 Amsterdam Candidates Tournament held in the Netherlands witnessed ten of the best masters in the world compete for top honours. This eighteen-round classical and elite tournament would offer the winner a chance to be the challenger for the next World Championship match. Armenian-Soviet grandmaster Tigran Petrosian was one of the exciting players who had emerged on the scene. He was much talked about as he had reached the grandmaster title from the 'Candidate' master title in only six years. But Tigran Petrosian flattered only to deceive. He had a disastrous start, losing his round 1 game to Russian grandmaster Efim Geller. In round 2, he faced another Russian grandmaster named David Bronstein.

Tigran Petrosian looked all set to win the game with a positional advantage over his opponent Bronstein. Not only that, Bronstein had also let his clock run to a point where it had become impossible for him to make four moves without crossing the time limit. That's when Petrosian made the blunder in a rapid move by putting his queen en prise for nothing. With his last move, Nf5, he had threatened his opponent's queen. But in his next move, instead of removing the queen, Petrosian played the baffling Ng5. Then he played Nd6 and resigned from the game immediately afterwards. This was a double error of sorts by Petrosian as his first mistake wouldn't have affected the outcome of the game then. But he was so shocked having made that blunder that he resigned from the game, completely forgetting about the hopeless time situation of Bronstein. It was the silliest double blunder in chess.

3. Sergey Karjakin

The annual Corus Tournament has now been renamed the Tata Steel Masters. The 2005 Corus Chess Tournament was held in Wijk aan Zee in the Netherlands and was divided into several groups based on the skill levels of the players. In group B, one of the promising new talents competing with the veterans was fifteen-year-old Russian Grandmaster Sergey Karjakin, a powerful young player. In 2003, Karjakin became the youngest grandmaster aged twelve years and seven months. Group B had big names in chess like Shakhriyar Mamedyarov, Peter Heine Nielsen and Magnus Carlsen, but that didn't bother Karjakin at all who was itching to make a mark on the world stage. He started off brilliantly and after eleven rounds had 8.5 points under his belt without losing a single game. Then in Sergey Karjakin's round 12 game, a strange thing happened. He faced Danish grandmaster Peter Heine Nielsen, who only had 6/11 at that stage. The two players played a normal and safe game that was heading towards a draw. But in the hundredth move of the game, which was a silly Kg5, White just took the rook on in the counter move with Na1, forcing Karjakin to resign.

4. Surya Shekhar Ganguly

The 2023 FIDE World Rapid and Blitz Championships took place in Samarkhand, Uzbekistan. Magnus Carlsen won both the Rapid and Blitz. Indian grandmaster Surya Shekhar Ganguly was one of the powerful representatives from India, but has disappeared from the chess scene after this competition. When the competition began, it was clear that Surya wasn't in good form as he lost to several players lower rated than him. Upon entering round 8, Surya was only at 3.5/7. Thus, he had to now face a much lower rated player who was not even a grandmaster. Uzbek IM Mukhiddin Madaminov had a rating of 2415, which was 230 rating points below Surya. There Surya's opponent destroyed him in less than ten moves. Even though this was rapid chess, Ganguly's move of missing mate in the opening is one of the worst blunders by a grandmaster in chess history. It took just two minutes for the game to wrap up while Surya Shekhar Ganguly took thirteen seconds for his disastrous move 8 Nxe5.

5. Vladimir Kramnik

We have saved the best for last. The honours for the top blunder in chess history goes to Vladimir Kramnik. No, we are not talking about the error he made when he called Ding's blunder 'childish'. This is simply because he probably forgot his own gargantuan mistake that he made in 2006. It's been nineteen long years, so we thought we'll refresh his memory.

Vladimir Kramnik was the chosen one as the human representative who would duel with the lord of the machines. In 2006, World Chess Champion Vladimir Kramnik played a match with ChessBase chess computer Deep Fritz, billed as World Chess Challenge: Man vs Machine. However, no one remembers this match unlike Kasparov's epic duel with Deep Blue because of two things. The first is Kramnik's embarrassing loss to Deep Fritz and the second is because Kramnik destroyed his own reputation in chess circles after he accused some grandmasters like Hikaru Nakamura of cheating in online chess play. The match between Vladimir Kramnik and Deep Fritz was to feature six games held over a span of two weeks in Bonn, Germany. The first of the six games ended in a tame draw. But in the second game, a strange thing happened. Man and machine played a stale game to reach an endgame with a drawn queen and bishop versus a queen and knight. In the strangest blunder of all time in chess, Kramnik totally overlooked a checkmate in one move for Deep Fritz. Kramnik played 34.Qe3 to offer a queen exchange to Deep Fritz and the computer instantly played 35.Qh7 to find mate in one, which Kramnik completely missed.

But what did Russian chess legend and one of the icons of the game Garry Kasparov have to say about Gukesh's emergence as the youngest world champion ever? Former world champion Garry Kasparov had only words of praise for Gukesh. He said he was very impressed by Gukesh's temperament and declared that the Indian teenager was the deserving winner of the summit clash simply because he was better prepared than his Chinese counterpart Ding Liren. In a series of tweets on X, Kasparov summed up the situation perfectly using logic, reasoning and wit, some of the qualities he was best-known for during his undisputed reign as champion of the world.

'My congratulations to @DGukesh on his victory today. He has summitted the highest peak of all: making his mother happy!' Kasparov wrote on X in an emotional post that Gukesh and his mother will probably treasure for life.

'Gukesh impressively surmounted every obstacle and opponent in his path, especially considering his age, and nothing more can be asked. My thoughts on the historical world championship lineage with Magnus outside are known, but that is not the story today,' Kasparov added.

Garry Kasparov also differed with his honourable countrymen Kramnik and Filatov regarding the quality of play in the World Chess Championship summit clash between Gukesh and Ding.

'The level of play was quite high, at least equal to the previous match,' Kasparov wrote on X. 'Ding showed great resistance. As for the blunders, which world championship, or world champion, was without them? I had my share, and recall the double blunder in Carlsen-Anand 2014, g6. Matches take a toll,' Kasparov said.

Kasparov acknowledged Viswanathan Anand's contribution to Indian chess, saying, 'Gukesh was well-prepared and the player who played the best won the match. His victory caps a phenomenal year for India. Combined with Olympiad dominance, chess has returned to its cradle and the era of 'Vishy's children' is truly upon us!'

The term 'Vishy's children' has become a popular narrative in chess circles that has been propagated by former world champion Garry Kasparov and World No. 3 Hikaru Nakamura. It means that the present generation of chess prodigies from India like Gukesh, Praggnanandhaa and Arjun Erigaisi are 'Vishy's children' or 'Vishy's army'. The new generation of chess warriors from India are here to stay.

Kasparov summed up his series of tweets, saying, 'India is a nation with an unlimited pool of human talent, combined with the freedom to explore and develop it. The future is bright not only in chess. The summit has been reached and now the goal must be to raise it even higher for the next ascent. Congratulations again. Upward!'

Garry Kasparov defeated Anatoly Karpov in 1985 to become the youngest world chess champion at the time. Gukesh broke this record after defeating Ding Liren. It is only the greatest sportsmen who are happy when their records are broken in a sport as they realize that no one is bigger than the sport.

'Just noticed a coincidence that 12/12 is the 40th anniversary of one of my world championship milestones, winning my first game against Karpov in our first match in 1984, game 32! First step in salvaging my dignity in that one,' Kasparov recalled.

At the post-match press conference of the World Chess

Championship, Ding Liren was gracious in defeat and also spoke about his infamous and uncharacteristic Chinese blunder. 'I was totally in shock when I realized I had made a blunder. It took me some time to process it. I have no regrets though. Gukesh played brilliantly and deserved the victory,' he said. But the doubts and the questions raised still remained and the controversy rages on. 'How could Ding's move to f2 be a mere miscalculation or error?' experts argued. So, how did the newly crowned world champion respond to the criticism that was directed towards him for a title that he had deservedly won. Gukesh, unfazed by the criticism, admitted that the quality of some of the games might not have boasted of a high standard, but reiterated that only the possession of chess skills do not decide the outcome of world championship matches. 'It's also about character and willpower,' Gukesh stated confidently and calmly. His mentor Viswanathan Anand, advised Gukesh to ignore the negativity and barrage of criticism. 'It (criticism) comes with every match. To be honest, I think it just comes with the territory. You ignore it and that's all,' Anand said. Further, Anand said that Gukesh has risen to the top thanks to his consistent effort, hard work and dedication. He pointed out Gukesh's triumphs at the Candidates Tournament and the Chess Olympiad to emphasize that his victory over Ding was not a fluke.

'Such criticism is unavoidable for anyone who achieves greatness,' Anand concluded with golden words. 'You cannot expect to become world champion and not face some random criticism.'

QED!

First among Equals

Garry Kasparov

If a list is made on the top 3 chess players in the history of chess, there's one name which will probably be on everyone's list. The name is Kasparov, Garry Kasparov.

Born on 13 April 1963 in Azerbaijan, USSR, which was a part of the then Soviet Union, Garry Kasparov grew up in a city named Baku.

Garry fell in love with chess as a six-year-old and started playing the game. His passion for chess was discovered by his parents when he solved a particularly difficult chess problem. When Garry was thirteen, he won a Soviet youth championship. He won the World Junior Chess Championship in Germany in 1980 when he was seventeen years old to announce his arrival in chess. He became a grandmaster at the same time and qualified for the World Chess Championship in 1984. At the time, Garry Kasparov's Elo rating was 2851, which was the highest FIDE rating at the time in the history of chess before Magnus Carlsen broke the record later. Where Kasparov stands apart from the others is his reign as world champion for the highest consecutive years from 1986 to 2005, which is a remarkable achievement. In 1985, Kasparov achieved what was considered impossible when he beat the legendary Russian grandmaster Anatoly Karpov to become the youngest world champion at twenty-two, a record recently broken by Gukesh. Beating the legendary Anatoly Karpov was probably Garry Kasparov's toughest battle. The contest was high-octane as the first forty-eight games resulted in draws between the evenly matched opponents as youth fought with experience. Kasparov finally emerged triumphant to win the title with a score of 12.5–11.5, the slimmest margin possible. Karpov went down but not without a great fight! No wonder one of Garry Kasparov's books is titled *Kasparov vs Karpov* as a tribute to his battle with the great Anatoly Karpov.

Garry Kasparov could easily switch from being an aggressive player who attacked relentlessly to being reliant on positional play. Instead of calculating several moves in his mind like some modern players, Kasparov preferred to go with the flow, employing his creativity as the game progressed.

IBM produced a custom-built chess computer named Deep Blue. In 1996, Garry Kasparov played Deep Blue and emerged as the winner in a match that was popular across the world. Deep Blue got its revenge the next year when the rematch was held as Kasparov lost after resigning in the last game in the six matches played. Kasparov 1, Deep Blue 1.

All good things must come to an end, and it was no different with Kasparov. In 2000, he lost his World Chess Championship title to fellow Russian Vladimir Kramnik at the Braingames World Chess Championship. Kramnik won the title with a score of 8.5–6.5 after sixteen games were played between the two players. This was a famous victory as it ousted Kasparov from the top position after an astonishing fifteen years as the king of chess. Kasparov was still the highest-rated player in chess even after his loss. But after this defeat, Kasparov lost the urge for a comeback and finally announced his retirement from competitive chess in 2005.

Garry Kasparov in 1974 and 2015

4

TWO STATES

Avoid the crowd. Do your own thinking independently. Be the chess player, not the chess piece.
– Ralph Charell
(American author)

The controversy over Gukesh's win in the World Chess Championship had not yet subsided when another fresh wave of controversy rose in India. Was Gukesh Tamil or Telugu? This debate began when both the states of Tamil Nadu and Andhra Pradesh laid their claim on the Indian grandmaster Gukesh Dommaraju, each claiming that he was the son of the soil of their respective states. This sparked off a rivalry and cultural debate that can happen only in India. Even poor Gukesh is confused now.

The first gun in the state rivalry war was fired by the chief minister of Tamil Nadu, M.K. Stalin. Stalin posted his congratulations for Gukesh on X for his 'remarkable achievement' and stated that the victory solidified the status of Chennai as the global chess capital. Stalin's tweet included a photograph of him placing a gold medal around Gukesh's neck with the caption, 'Tamil Nadu is proud of you.'

Soon after Stalin's post, the chief minister of Andhra Pradesh, N. Chandrababu Naidu posted on X, claiming that Gukesh was 'our very own Telugu boy.'

Chess Excavations in India

- The oldest archaeological evidence of chess unearthed in India was highlighted by Professor Shikaripura Ranganatha Rao in his work *Lothal and Indus Civilization,* published in 1972. Professor S.R. Rao was an archaeologist from Karnataka and the leader of the teams that are credited with the discoveries of various sites in Harappa, like the port city of Lothal and Bet Dwarka in Gujarat. Chess pieces were discovered in Lothal which bore a close resemblance to the modern chess pieces we see today in terms of appearance, size and shape. These chess pieces from Lothal date back to 2450 BCE and were essentially animal-headed game pieces and pyramidal pieces with ivory handles.

- Excavations conducted in Tamil Nadu, Gukesh's home state, revealed chess pieces of a different kind. These were terracotta cylindrical pieces which were made from clay and burnt in a kiln.

- These were coloured red and black and had flat bottoms, most probably for easy handling and movement on the board.

His post read: 'Hearty congratulations to our very own Telugu boy, Indian Grandmaster D. Gukesh, on scripting history in

Singapore by becoming the world's youngest chess champion at just 18! The entire nation celebrates your incredible achievement. Wishing you many more triumphs and accolades in the decades to come.'

When the chief ministers of Tamil Nadu and Andhra Pradesh set the ball rolling to claim the eighteen-year-old world champion, even the netizens of the states jumped on the bandwagon to join the debate about Gukesh's Tamil–Telugu ancestry. Gukesh's roots are the main cause for this controversy. Gukesh was born and raised in Chennai, Tamil Nadu, but his parents have ties to Andhra Pradesh, and this has led to this tug of war of his origins. The online advocates of Tamil Nadu stated that Gukesh was born and raised in Tamil Nadu and hence no other state had the right to stake a claim to him. Also, the Tamil Nadu government had granted considerable support to the chess prodigy ever since his playing days to the present. One X user also posted a screenshot from April that stated that the Tamil Nadu government had given him a grant of ₹75 lakh. Online users from Andhra Pradesh argued why Gukesh is Telugu and not Tamil. They stated that as his roots were Telugu, his Tamil Nadu domicile could not dilute his Telugu roots in any manner possible.

Instead of this parochial bickering, it's time to celebrate Gukesh and his team, which includes his Polish coach and main second Grzegorz Gajewski, Grandmasters Jan-Krzysztof Duda (rapid chess expert), Jan Klimkowski and Radosław Wojtaszek also from Poland, Vincent Keymer from Germany and Indian Grandmaster Pentala Harikrishna. South African Paddy Upton was Gukesh's mental trainer and offered his expertise in mental conditioning to enhance Gukesh's psychological resilience, which was the key to his World Chess Championship success.

Chaturanga

The game of chess was called chaturanga in ancient India and came into existence nearly 1,500 years ago during the reign of the Gupta Empire. The sixth century saw the game becoming really popular across India. The name 'chaturanga' was taken from the four divisions of the military such as the infantry, cavalry, elephantry and chariotry. These are reflective of the modern-day pawn, knight, rook and bishop which are the pieces that play key roles in the game of chess. The game involved battle simulation which is reflective of the military strategy that existed. The battle formations from the famous Indian epic of Mahabharata have also shaped two important features of chaturanga, which are that all the different pieces possess different powers and that victory was solely dependent on the king's survival.

India's considerable mathematical advancement during the ancient and medieval times gave birth to the revolutionary design of the original chessboard. The chessboard was based on the wheat and chessboard problem, and the game itself was designed for an 'ashtapada', an 8x8 square playing board which was named after the spider in the Sanskrit language, the arachnid with eight legs. There were other Indian boards like the 10x10 'dasapada' and the 9x9 'saturankam'. The ashtapada was the most popular. However, there were no black and white squares on these boards for thousands of years.

The Legend Behind the Wheat Chessboard Problem

Once upon a time, there was an Indian king named Shihram who was notorious as a tyrant. This king had a wise man in his court who had supposedly invented the game of chess with a sole purpose. He wished to transform the king and display to him that everyone else was equally important in the kingdom, no matter how small or insignificant. The wise man presented his invention before the king and explained how each of the chess pieces worked. He explained that just like the king in the game of chess, a king in real life also needed the support and strength of his queen, rooks, bishops, knights and pawns for his safety and survival and that of the kingdom. The king understood what the wise man was trying to say and promised to change for the better. He was so pleased with the wise man for his brilliant invention that he wanted to reward him with gold, silver and other riches. But the wise man refused to accept any valuables and instead made a strange request to the king. He asked the king to place one grain of wheat on the first square, two grains on the second square, and keep doubling up the wheat till the last square on the chessboard was covered. When the king tried to fill the chessboard according to the wise man's instructions, he was amazed to realize that this was an impossible task. This was because the chessboard had been designed in such a unique way that the mathematical exponent summed up to become a staggering amount of 1,84,46,744 trillion of wheat grains. The granaries of his kingdom did not possess so much grain. Why, no kingdom could fulfil such an incredible requirement!

The king finally understood what the wise man was trying to say. Wealth could not buy everything, especially this brilliant invention, which was one in a millennium. From that day onwards, this king respected all the people in his kingdom and from a tyrant became a just and kind ruler. He also became addicted to the game of chess and encouraged everyone in his kingdom to play it. He also ensured that the popularity of chess spread to faraway lands.

Viswanathan Anand was Gukesh's mentor and idol since his early days. But the story behind how German Grandmaster Vincent Keymer joined Gukesh's team for the World Championship is an interesting one. Keymer was Gukesh's rival and Gukesh admired the German grandmaster for his great understanding of chess and amazing knowledge of chess openings. During the 2024 Candidates Tournament, Gukesh suffered a humiliating defeat at the hands of Alireza Firouzja in round 7. Keymer sent Gukesh a long WhatsApp message after this loss to cheer him up and support him. This show of support and solidarity at this crucial juncture moved Gukesh as Keymer was his rival after all. When Gukesh was discussing his choice of seconds with his coach Grzegorz Gajewski, he casually mentioned the WhatsApp message sent by Keymer. The Polish coach came up with the suggestion the very next day that Keymer should join Gukesh's team as his second. Gukesh was agreeable to the idea, and when Keymer was approached, he agreed as well. Thus, Vincent Keymer became a part of the team that would help Gukesh become the champion of the world.

Gukesh's father Dr Rajinikanth credited a senior Indian grandmaster for playing a big role in his son's growth as a chess player: Harikrishna, a thirty-eight-year-old grandmaster from Andhra Pradesh who helped Gukesh with his chess moves for a week in 2022. This led to Gukesh winning tournaments like the Gijon Open and the Chennai Olympiad. It also enhanced his ratings as he crossed 2700 Elo in Biel. The one-week intense camp at Harikrishna's house helped Gukesh strengthen his game and move upwards to qualify for the World Championship. In 2016, Grandmaster Harikrishna reached a peak world ranking of 10, and he had an impressive Elo rating of 2770 in the same year. Gukesh attributed his success to this core team.

Gukesh had special words reserved in praise for his longtime

A second is another player who helps a competitor prepare for a match. Generally this trusted advisor is a first-rate player who helps the competitor build a strategy, analyse the opponent's strengths and weaknesses, provide psychological support and even predict likely moves for a forthcoming match.

idol and mentor, the one and only Viswanathan Anand. As soon as Gukesh landed in Chennai from Singapore on 16 December 2024 and found some free time, he thanked the most famous Indian grandmaster on his official X account. Gukesh hailed Vishy Sir as his inspiration and idol from the beginning of his chess playing days and also stated that he learnt a lot from him during their discussions on chess.

Gukesh at Chennai Book Fair 2025

FIDE profile – Gukesh as on 20 February 2025					
World Rank (Active)	**Federation**	**Fide ID**	**B-year**	**Sex**	**FIDE Title**
5	India	46616543	2006	Male	GM

FIDE rating in all 3 formats

Standard	Rapid	Blitz
2777	2654	2615

*GM: GRANDMASTER

Transformation of **Chess**

As chess migrated from India to other parts of the world, it witnessed several changes in its format. The 'elephant' was transformed into the 'camel' in the Middle-Eastern and Persian versions of the game. Different chess pieces in Europe were introduced, such as the 'fool' in France and the 'bishop' in England. The 'horse' was transformed into the 'knight'. Sometimes, even a ship was used as a chess piece, and this could have been because of the Persian influence on the game or because of the maritime influence of coastal India.

5

GUKESH AND MAGNUS CARLSEN – THE BATTLE FOR CHESS SUPREMACY

All that matters on the chessboard is good moves.
– Bobby Fischer
(American chess grandmaster)

After his tremendous achievement in winning the World Chess Championship, Gukesh did not have much time to celebrate his monumental feat. He headed to the Netherlands to participate in the prestigious Tata Steel Chess 2025 Masters, held in Wijk aan Zee. This tournament is known in the chess circuit as the 'Wimbledon of Chess' tournaments. It's also one of the famed trio of major tournaments in which Gukesh had intended to leave a mark by performing well and silence his critics who are of the opinion that the quality of play in the World Championship was below par when one equated it to previous world championship standards. However, the margin in competitive chess is a rather thin one. In a stunning finale, Gukesh went down to fellow Indian R. Praggnanandhaa, or Praggs, who clinched this title. After his win, Praggs said that Gukesh's triumph at the World Championship had inspired him to work harder.

Gukesh's triumph in Singapore sent social media in a frenzy as he was applauded by both previous and current grandmasters for his remarkable achievement of being the youngest player ever to be crowned the world champion. But mixed reactions were received from some grandmasters as well, including the current great Magnus Carlsen. In 2003, the Norwegian chess grandmaster decided to abdicate the world crown after being on top for ten years. So he decided not to defend his world championship title in 2023. Carlsen stated that the intense drudgery required for months to prepare for a title match were taking a toll on him both physically and mentally. Carlsen has also publicly said that he will never challenge Gukesh for the World Championship title. This was after Gukesh had stated that he would love a match-up with Carlsen in the near future.

'Winning the World Chess Championship does not mean I am the best player, obviously that is Magnus Carlsen,' Gukesh confessed with his characteristic humility. 'I want to reach the level Magnus has achieved. Obviously playing against Magnus in the world championship would be amazing; it would be the toughest challenge there is in chess. It is up to Magnus, but I would love to test myself against the best player in the world.'

Top 10 Chess Players – February 2025			
Rank	Name	Federation	Rating
1	Magnus Carlsen	Norway	2833
2	Fabiano Caruana	USA	2803
3	Hikaru Nakamura	USA	2802
4	Arjun Erigaisi	India	2801
5	Gukesh Dommaraju	India	2777
6	Nodirbek Abdusattorov	Uzbekistan	2766
7	Alireza Firouzja	France	2760
8	Wei Yi	China	2755
9	Ian Nepomniachtchi	Russia	2754
10	Viswanathan Anand	India	2750

Magnus Carlsen has also ruled out the prospect of playing the World Chess Championship. 'I am not part of this circus anymore,' Carlsen said, referring to world title clashes. However, chess fans need not be disappointed. The two grandmasters did clash at the Freestyle Chess Grand Slam Tour in February. But before that a little more of how Carlsen analysed Gukesh's performance at the World Chess Championship.

'It's a really good thing for him, he has the title now for two years, winning this championship is extremely motivating, so there is a very good chance that he is going to go for a great run of results now and probably become the number two player now and may be number one in the not so distant future,' Magnus Carlsen stated after analysing the title match. Carlsen also praised Gukesh's team for the good job in helping him reach his goal.

'It is becoming progressively harder (to play mainstream openings) all main lines are analysed so they had to jump a bit,' Magnus Carlsen said of the opening choices made by Gukesh. 'I have generally kept it fairly risk-free with the white pieces, I have tried not to let things go out of control,' he added. However, Carlsen was also critical of Gukesh's style of play. He wrote: 'If Gukesh was playing Fabiano Caruana or Hikaru Nakamura in this match and played the same way, he would probably have had a very difficult time.'

It is worth noting that both Caruana and Nakamura, American grandmasters and World No. 2 and 3 respectively, were edged out by just half a point at the Toronto Candidates Tournament held in April, when Gukesh qualified as the challenger and triumphed. But Carlsen also feels that Gukesh has the potential to win tournaments to become No. 2 after him or even beat him and become No. 1. Gukesh, on the other hand, regards the Norwegian superstar as his idol and confesses that Carlsen is still ahead of him so far as talent is concerned. But then again, didn't Gukesh say that it is not talent alone that wins a tournament? 'It's a motivating factor, trying to reach the level of greatness that Magnus has achieved,' Gukesh said. But what this really means is that Gukesh will go all out in his attempts to replicate Magnus Carlsen's incredible achievements until his mandatory title defence in 2026.

The world will be watching.

Meanwhile, at the Freestyle Chess Grand Tour in Weissenhaus, Germany, Gukesh had to face Carlsen in the last match of the round-robin stage (where all players play one another, in contrast to elimination rounds). The match surely saw some interesting moves from both the giants, but Gukesh flattered to deceive. He made a blunder with his knight in round 9, and Carlsen won the match. Gukesh, nonetheless, stayed in the fray. On 10 February 2025, Gukesh lost to USA's Fabiano Caruana – resigning in eighteen moves. This finally knocked him out of the tournament.

The year 2025 will see another clash between these two great champions when they meet in Norway Chess at Stavanger in May–June. Then there's the Sinquefield Cup at St. Louis in August. But the invited field for this tournament has not yet been announced yet. Chess fans are optimistic of a duel between Carlsen and Gukesh here as well. Polish grandmaster and D. Gukesh's coach Grzegorz Gajewski has drawn an interesting

> Even as he lost, Gukesh taught us a mighty lesson in life. He maintained a heart rate of 78 BPM even at the crunch, when for Caruana, the winner of the match, it rose to 124 BPM at a similar situation.

comparison between his protégé and five-time world champion Magnus Carlsen who many chess fans consider the greatest chess player of all time. Gajewski feels that the styles of both players have a clear distinction. He feels that Gukesh's analytical approach on the chessboard is what makes him different from Carlsen, who is more reliant on intuitive gameplay. 'He will never be a player like Magnus Carlsen in the sense of being an intuitive kind of a player,' Gajewski said about Gukesh. 'He likes to calculate and he likes to go deep into position. He doesn't like to make moves just purely based on intuition. He will never play in the Magnus style, but he can very well mimic it.'

But Magnus Carlsen's assessment of Gukesh's style of play before he won the World Chess Championship is interesting as the man who lost to Gukesh, Ding Liren, probably also shared the same opinion, and it didn't end too well for him, did it? This is what Carlsen had said: 'Greatness will come to Gukesh if he can master rapid & blitz chess, where he's ranked 46 and 82.'

Amazing Facts about **Magnus Carlsen**

- Magnus Carlsen was born on 30 November 1990, in Tønsberg, Norway. Just like the great rapid chess that he is renowned for, his rise to become a grandmaster in chess was equally rapid. Magnus Carlsen is regarded by many to be the greatest chess player ever to play the game because of his sharp mind, strategic skills and amazing abilities to anticipate his opponent's moves. The icing on the cake is his glorious achievements and titles in international chess. Thanks to Carlsen, chess has evolved into a global sport. But here are some lesser-known facts about the great Magnus Carlsen that are equally amazing.

- Before he became fascinated with chess, Carlsen was obsessed with Lego at an early age. As a toddler, he displayed early signs of skills like problem-solving and creativity and made his own designs. This love affair with Lego led to the growth of two main skills – attention to detail and the enhancing of spatial reasoning – which helped him become a great chess player.

- Magnus Carlsen has been blessed with a photographic memory. He can easily recall specific moves and strategies, some of which are from games he played several years ago, right to the precise placement of precise pieces made on the chessboard. He also uses his photographic memory to store details he likes from day-to-day events, literature, movies and other aspects of popular culture. This incredible memory gives him an edge over his rivals, as he remembers their strengths and weaknesses and has access to a treasure trove of information and data throughout the course of a chess match.

- Despite his celebrity status, Magnus Carlsen is a simple man who's pretty grounded. He often plays informal chess with common people in places like public parks, where he freely interacts with amateur players and provides them tips and strategies to help their game. He also gives them an opportunity to play chess against a world champion. This helps him keep in touch with amateur chess and also displays his sheer love for the game and the fans.

- Carlsen loves music and his favourite genres are Western classical and electronic music. He has said that music helps him focus and acts as a diversion from the pressure of competitive chess.

- Magnus Carlsen is a self-confessed football fan, and is a supporter of his local Lyn Football Club and the Spanish giants Real Madrid. He has said that if he hadn't pursued a career in chess, he would have liked to become a professional footballer. In his spare time, the Norwegian loves playing football and also participates in local games and competitions, playing as a midfielder. Why aren't we surprised that he is a playmaker? Carlsen also loves playing fantasy football and enjoys the strategy that's involved in the entire process. He likes monitoring player output, studying game data and takes crucial decisions involving his fantasy team. One can gauge the immense strategic abilities Magnus Carlsen possesses as he led the Fantasy Premier League standings briefly in the 2019–2020 season. This obsession with fantasy football has further enhanced his tactical planning skills and love for data.

- Carlsen also loves playing video games. He enjoys playing poker and loves playing high-stakes games with his close friends. A poker face surely helps a chess player!

- In 2010, Magnus Carlsen shocked chess purists when he joined the fashion industry to co-model for Dutch apparel line G-Star Raw with actress and model Liv Tyler. That did raise a lot of eyebrows in chess circles, but it was a smart move that put him in the spotlight and created more fans outside the chess world, thanks to mainstream media.

- Last but not the least, Carlsen is a huge environmental advocate and has campaigned to spread awareness about climate change using his celebrity status. Collaborations with environmental groups like WWF and Greenpeace have helped him endorse items that are eco-friendly and sustainable measures such as the reduction of plastic use.

Magnus Carlsen

Top 10 Chess Tactics

of the Great

Anatoly Karpov

Born on 23 May 1951, Anatoly Karpov holds the reputation of being one of the strongest players in chess history. He held the title of world champion from 1975 to 1985 and reigned as No. 1 player of the world for 102 months at a stretch. The surprising element in Karpov's style of play was that he appeared to win his games with effortless ease, without any display of striking moves. However, there is more to it than meets the eye as Karpov was armed with certain secret weapons which have been analysed in detail below.

♟ **PROPHYLAXIS**

Prophylaxis might sound complicated but is actually not, and is something that's been happening for centuries in both war and sport. It basically means playing against your opponent's ideas and taking a moment to halt them before executing your own plans. This was typical of Anatoly Karpov, and he was notorious for this uncomfortable (for the opponent, of course) style of play.

♟ **RESTRICTING THE OPPONENT'S ACTIVE PLAY**

This strategy is linked closely to prophylaxis

or prophylactic play. But restricting the opponent's play is keeping the opponent tied up by not allowing him any room for counter-play to gain any advantage in the game. Karpov employed this difficult defensive manoeuvre naturally and effortlessly. He was most famous for his boaconstrictor style of play in which he squeezed his opponents dry and pushed them up against the wall as soon as he gained the slightest advantage.

- **HANDLING STATIC POSITIONS**
  Hedgehog structure in chess is probably one of the most difficult positions to play as nothing has to be changed here. One cannot make any changes in the pawn structure or make any unnecessary pawn moves. This is not an easy thing to do for any chess player, but Anatoly Karpov handled static positions brilliantly.

- **DEFENSIVE PLAY**
  Karpov's defensive play was solid as he was good even when he was in a bad position to emerge from the threat unscathed. As he could handle static positions without breaking into a sweat, Karpov was naturally good when he was pushed against the wall. Passive play was a unique Karpov trait.

- **MANOEUVRES**
  Karpov made crucial manoeuvres which he innovated on as the game progressed.

He employed inventive techniques to play creatively and always improve his pieces on the chessboard.

♟ **POSITIONAL PLAY**

Anatoly Karpov was a master of positional play and could give a masterclass on handling different types of pawn structures, the isolated or hanging pawns for example.

♟ **PATIENCE**

Karpov was an extremely patient player who was not in a hurry to win the game even though he had wrested the advantage from his opponent. Instead, he took his time to create additional pressure on his opponent. Patience, as they say, is a virtue.

♟ **PLAYING WITH THE OPPOSITE-COLOURED BISHOPS**

Karpov's superior technique was perhaps best reflected in positions with opposite-coloured bishops, where his play was magical. During middlegames or complex endgames, he used his bishops with great precision and skill to outsmart his opponents.

♟ **THE CARO-KANN**

Karpov also had some of the best openings in chess. The Caro-Kann was one of his favourite openings and he also made some important theoretical contributions to this particular chess opening.

THE QUEEN'S INDIAN

The Queen's Indian was another opening that was typically Karpov. This was a safe and solid opening to begin the game.

Anatoly Karpov, Russian chess grandmaster and former world champion during his visit to Serbia in 2016

6

THE PREDICTIONS: BEFORE AND AFTER

The best way to predict the future
is to create it on the chessboard.
– Garry Kasparov
(Russian chess grandmaster)

The buzz around Gukesh in chess circles is optimistic, and general consensus is that the eighteen-year-old world champion will only improve his overall game in the years to come. However, his present style is over-dependent on strategy and lacks the creativity needed at the top level. There are small gaps and weaknesses in unclear positions that experienced grandmasters might breach easily in a crunch game as suggested by Magnus Carlsen.

Also, closer examination of chess history data reveals that it's not necessary that a grandmaster improves between the late teens and the early twenties, and that makes this theory of Gukesh becoming a better player over the years a kind of wishful thinking. Take the case of the famous American grandmaster Bobby Fischer, for example. When Fischer announced his arrival at the world stage by winning the Stockholm Interzonal in the spring of 1962 as a nineteen-year-old, he was the talk of the chess circles. Although a hot favourite to win the Candidates after that, Fischer failed to do so and became world champion only ten years later.

When a nineteen-year-old Boris Spassky was third in the 1956 Candidates, it was predicted that he would be the next challenger to the throne. But the predictions went wrong when his career stalled and he had to wait for more than a decade to win the world championship and wear the crown on his head. The competition in global chess is as good as it gets and anything can happen. In recent times, an eighteen-year-old Alireza Firouzja became the youngest player in chess history to achieve a rating of 2800. But contrary to expectations, he failed to impress in two consecutive Candidates tournaments. Hence, Gukesh's future cannot be predicted with absolute certainty just yet. It remains to be seen whether his reign as world champion will be short lived or as illustrious as some of his famous predecessors. Gukesh has himself expressed confidence that he will have a career that's both long and successful. The truth will be revealed with the speed of rapid chess in just a year's time.

But as far as predictions in chess go, there's no one more likely to be most accurate than the grandmasters themselves. Even when the FIDE World Championship was in progress, American grandmaster Maurice Ashley was impressed watching Gukesh in action. But Ashley feels that Gukesh has not reached his peak yet, and this will come in another ten years' time. This is a positive prediction as Ashley feels that Gukesh will reach heights that hasn't been scaled by anyone before. Indian grandmasters Pravin Thipsay and Abhijit Kunte had predicted even before the World Championship that Gukesh would beat his Chinese opponent Ding Liren by the twelfth round. Although it took a couple of rounds more than that, this prediction was almost accurate as Gukesh did not disappoint. But this prediction was based mostly on chess data more than anything else. Gukesh had a terrific run in 2024 while Ding failed to win a game in the classical format the entire year. Thipsay based his prediction on the fact that Gukesh does not make any mistakes for his opponent to gain the advantage and felt that despite being fourteen years younger than Ding, he was a more mature chess player.

> This was reflected in the game as Gukesh held his nerve and remained calm while Ding started crying after losing the fourth game.

Thipsay felt the difference would be in the strength of character between the two players, and he was proved right. He thought Gukesh possessed a strength of character very similar to that of Anatoly Karpov. Even his style of play resembles that of the Russian great. Kunte was in awe of Gukesh's work ethics, stating that whatever he did in life was with the sole aim of improving his chess play more than anything else.

'So like if he is resting, it is also because he needs a rest to improve his chess. If he is reading, he is reading because it will help him to improve his chess. Whatever he does, it finally focuses on how he is improving his chess,' Kunte explained, and gave credit to Gukesh's parents and coaches for providing him with a platform on which he could lay the foundation of his success. Kunte also gave an important reason why he favoured Gukesh to beat Ding. He said that Ding was not the player he was before after his battle against depression.

'We have like Ding era one and Ding era two. Right now he is in Ding two which is not very strong. But if you see Ding one, it was very difficult to beat him,' Kunte explained.

Indian grandmasters Pravin Thipsay and Abhijit Kunte haven't predicted what lies in store for Gukesh next. But after their spot-on prediction for the World Championship, we certainly wouldn't mind finding out.

How **Chess Travelled**

Chess travelled with the speed of a freight train after its origins in northern India and caught on like a rage across India. Then it travelled to Persia and spread across the land. The first mention of the game in Persia is in the seventh-century Persian history, *Artakhshatr-i-Papakan*. Its Persian designation 'shatranj' comes from Sanskrit 'chaturaṅga'. Chess invaded China during the reign of the Han Dynasty. When the Muslims conquered Persia, they were introduced to chess and were instantly hooked. They adapted the game into their culture, and during the Moorish conquest of Spain, chess entered Europe and soon became a popular sport.

As Gukesh embarks on his difficult journey in an attempt to add more illustrious feathers to his crown, he faces significant challenges from both older and contemporary rivals. All of them are focused to try and win the 2026 Candidates Tournament and then go all out to dethrone the young Indian champion from the top seat. The reigning US champion, thirty-two-year-old Italian-American grandmaster Fabiano Caruana, is not far away from securing his 2026 spot, having already won the recent US Masters and the St. Louis Masters. He had been close to the world crown in both 2018 and 2024, and looks certain to book his place in the 2026 Candidates. Closer to home, Gukesh faces stiff challenges from twenty-one-year-old Indian grandmaster Arjun Erigaisi, who is currently the World No. 4 and is considered Gukesh's main Indian rival in the international scheme of things.

It is noteworthy that Arjun Erigaisi and Rameshbabu Praggnanandhaa were Gukesh's main colleagues on India's gold medal Olympiad team. Did they stay away from helping Gukesh when he faced Ding? And if that is the case, is it because none of the two Indian grandmasters wanted to spoil their chances in the future as they also aspired for the world title. By helping Gukesh, they may have ended up giving away all their opening secrets as well as their key strategies. The stage is set for an interesting battle ahead.

> In fact, Viswanathan Anand has already predicted there is a slim chance of about 5–10 per cent that there will be a face-off between Gukesh and the Warangal chess prodigy Arjun Erigaisi in the 2026 World Chess Championship.

Erigaisi has been in top form in 2024 and has secured his place in the Top 5 rankings, which is a commendable feat.

In the beginning of 2024, Erigaisi's FIDE live ratings were around 2740. But during the course of the year, Erigaisi crossed the 2800 mark and is now the second Indian after Anand, the former world champion, to officially go past this rating barrier. No wonder Anand has so much faith in Erigaisi to come up trumps. In October 2024, Erigaisi beat Russian grandmaster Dmitry Andreikin in round five of the European Chess Club Cup in Serbia to reach a live rating of 2802.1. He only became the sixteenth player in the history of chess to be a part of this exclusive club. India No. 1 Arjun Erigaisi had already predicted before the World Championship that his teammate Gukesh would beat his Chinese opponent. After Gukesh lifted the world title, Erigaisi said, 'Gukesh's achievement is massive and I am very happy for him. The result was not a surprise in any way, but it was a pleasant surprise to see it happen today as it looked like it was going to head into playoffs.'

Right now, Arjun Erigaisi has challenges of his own. The road ahead is tough for Erigaisi, but he doesn't want to think ahead as he believes these are still early days for permutations and combinations. Instead, he insisted that everyone should celebrate Gukesh's historic feat. 'I think we should all just enjoy Gukesh's victory for now,' Arjun Erigaisi said famously.

The stellar moment in Erigaisi's career was beating Magnus Carlsen, who is considered the best chess player of this era and also the greatest ever by many. But the manner of the victory was surprising as Magnus Carlsen was blown away by Erigaisi in a blitz game in only twenty moves and in under six minutes. This took place at the Tata Steel Chess India tournament in Kolkata, India, and this was Magnus Carlsen's first loss in seventeen games across raid and blitz formats.

But the battle for chess supremacy has many contenders as Erigaisi discovered in the Chennai Grandmasters when Aravindh Chithambaram defeated him to win the title. And his Candidates 2026 qualification hopes crashed when an eighteen-year-old Russian, Volodar Murzin, won the FIDE World Rapid Championship in New York on 29 December 2024. The buzz at the Tata Steel Chess India tournament in Kolkata, however, was not about Magnus Carlsen but an Indian player who idolized him. This chess player from Kolkata the world's youngest-rated with FIDE ratings of 1555 after having played five rated players. His name is Anish Sarkar and he was only three years old then. This kid met his idol Magnus Carlsen in Kolkata, who praised Anish to the skies.

The Origin of the Name
Chess

When a form of chaturanga spread from India to Persia, the Persian kings changed the name of the Sanskrit 'rajah' to the Persian 'shah'. The Persians called checkmate 'shahmat'. After chess spread across Europe, the Germans called it 'shach', which meant 'the game of the kings'. Then the term 'eches' was coined by the French, which meant 'to fail'. The English version of 'eches' is chess. This is the name that stuck.

There is a high probability that Anish Sarkar could go on to become the youngest grandmaster in chess history. In a context where the youngest world champion in chess history has been crowned from India, this will be another glorious feather in India's cap. But then again, that's also a prediction that has to stand the test of time.

Strangely, Gukesh's mentor Viswanathan Anand did not think that Gukesh had it in him to become a future challenger when he was in his early teens. Anand was of the opinion that Gukesh did not possess enough experience to make it to the top. Today, Anand must be more than happy to be proven wrong. He expressed his great pride in seeing his student's incredible transformation over the years.

'It's a golden generation of Indian players establishing themselves at the top,' Anand declared. This is absolutely spot on as Gukesh is at the apex of a robust chess ecosystem in India, which is arguably the best in the world. India has over 85 grandmasters, 120 international masters and tens of thousands of rated players now, and many among them haven't yet reached driving age. The Indian chess ecosystem of the twenty-first century is reminiscent of the decades of the Soviet Union's dominance in chess.

Even before the World Championship, Gukesh had made it clear that he didn't think about predictions. His job was to go out there and play good chess. He said that if he did that, he believed good things would happen. His focus was entirely on the job at hand and he was well aware that he would have to go out there and play at his best. Right said champ!

FUN CHESS FACTS

- Chess is a mandatory school subject in Armenia.

- About 70 per cent of the adult population has played chess at some point in their lives. Approximately 605 million people play chess on a regular basis. There are over 700 million chess players in the world.

- In a single game of chess, there are 400 possible moves after each move is played.

- The year 1090 CE saw the first chessboard with alternating light and dark squares appear in Europe.

- The oldest surviving complete chess sets were discovered on the Isle of Lewis in Northern Scotland and date back to the twelfth century. These were most likely made in Norway or Iceland. The appearance of these chess sets was used in the famous Hollywood blockbuster *Harry Potter and the Sorcerer's Stone* for the chess pieces of the wizard.

- Before 1600, a game of chess could be won by capturing all of the opponent's pieces, leaving just a bare king alone on the chessboard. This ruthless style of play was called 'annihilation'. In medieval times, players considered it nobler to win by checkmate, and the concept of annihilation was slowly abandoned. This style of play still holds good to date.

- A man invented a machine in 1770 that he claimed could play a strong game of chess against a human opponent. The wonderful invention was named 'the Turk'. It was not till 1854 that the entire episode was revealed to be a hoax after it was discovered that a chess master was hiding inside the machine.

- It sure took a long time for the Turk to be exposed after exhibitions in Europe and the United States. Eighty-four years to be precise!

- Chess clocks were first used in chess in 1883, and the first world chess championship was held three years later, in 1886.

- During World War II, some of the top chess players also served as code breakers. British chess masters Harry Golombek, Stuart Milner-Barry and Hugh O'Doncl Alexander were on the team which broke the Nazi Enigma code.

- Dr Emanuel Lasker from Germany retained the title of world chess champion longer than any other player in the world ever. He held the title for an astonishing 26 years and 337 days.

- The world record for the most number of moves without capture was set in 1992 and involved 100 moves.

- You can checkmate your opponent in just two moves.

- It has been proved that chess can improve memory function.

- The longest official game of chess took place in 1989. The marathon game continued for twenty hours and fifteen minutes. It featured 269 moves and ended in a draw.

- The year 1999 saw Garry Kasparov versus the rest of the world in chess. Grandmaster Kasparov played against more than fifty thousand people belonging to more than seventy-five countries in a single game of chess that lasted for over four months. The moves of the opponents were decided by majority vote. Kasparov won the game on turn 62 when 51 per cent of his worldly opponents decided to resign.

7

THE HUMILITY AND SIMPLICITY OF A CHAMPION

Becoming successful at chess allows you to discover your own personality. That's what I want for the kids I teach.
– Saudin Robovic
(International master, Bosnia and Herzegovina)

Amidst all the euphoria and the celebrations following Gukesh's famous victory in the FIDE World Championship, what stands out is his humility in the wake of such an achievement. In an era when champions in sports leave no stone unturned in posing for photographs with the championship trophy, celebrating with the trophy in wild abandon and gusto with some also going to sleep in the night clutching the trophy close to them or keeping it by their bedside, Gukesh is a bit different from the others. For starters, he said he did not want to touch the world championship trophy after his victory or celebrate it. He said he would prefer to wait till the official ceremony, when he touched the trophy and lifted it. For someone who dreamed of his glorious moment since he was seven years old, and had waited patiently for so many years to achieve this dream, Gukesh didn't mind waiting a little longer to get his hands on the coveted trophy and doing everything the official way. That's what makes him special as everything he does is disciplined, meticulous and practical. The manner in which he religiously arranges the pieces on the chessboard after every game, regardless of the result, is testimony to his character and humility. He never lets his emotions get the better of him although this win moved him to tears because of the culmination of a childhood dream. The eighteen-year-old did have a smile on his face as he cast lovelorn glances at the trophy after his victory. After winning, Gukesh displayed his humility by praising his opponent Ding Liren at the closing ceremony of the World Chess Championship. He said that Ding was a true champion whom he admired. Humility after victory is a rare trait. Gukesh is also the shining example of simple living and high thinking. When asked how the new world champion felt after becoming a multi-millionaire, as he's now richer by ₹11.5 crore because of the prize money he received after winning the World Championship, Gukesh was quick to reply that money wasn't the reason why he played chess and that he treasured this journey more than the wealth it fetched him. But Gukesh must be relieved it all worked out as his parents made a lot of sacrifices and faced hardships so that he could make this incredible journey and follow his dreams. Gukesh's father gave up a rewarding career as an ENT surgeon so that he could accompany his son on his circuit tours, while Gukesh's mother, a microbiologist, served as the breadwinner of the family by working doubly hard. Gukesh's humility and simplicity stems from his upbringing as his parents have raised him so well. Gukesh has simple goals in life as well although they won't be simple to achieve for sure. He wants to be the best chess player in the world by displacing Magnus Carlsen from the pole position. He also wants to have a long and successful career at the top. The world championship title might be the beginning of this illustrious career. At least that's what all Indian fans will be collectively hoping for. An event perfectly illustrates that the world champion is also a simple, fun-loving teenager despite all that discipline. After winning the world championship, Gukesh went bungee jumping with his trainer Gajewski to honour a promise made. During one of the rest days after game 9 of the gruelling match, Gukesh and his trainer went for a walk on the beach to de-stress. They saw people bungee jumping there and Gajewski declared that he would jump off that bridge too if Gukesh defeated Ding. Gukesh responded that he would do the same if he managed to win despite his fear of heights. After winning against Ding, Gukesh thought both he and his trainer should honour the deal they had made on the beach. So both of them went bungee jumping for the first time in their lives, and probably their last.

Gukesh must have realized that he should conquer all his fears, especially his fear of heights if he wanted to reach the top!

Gukesh exudes a confidence and maturity way beyond his age. He turns up well-dressed for his chess games with a sacred white dot on his forehead. He never boasts or talks big either before or after a game and never celebrates wildly after a victory. The world championship triumph was a notable exception when we saw a hint of celebrations, albeit subdued. There is no thumping of chests like superstars in other sports like cricket or football and there are no flying kisses blown to the audience like tennis stars. Considering his age, Gukesh seems to be cut from a different cloth altogether. Praising Ding after his victory displayed his humility, maturity and modesty in equal measure. Gukesh's upbringing and the positivity of traditional values has helped him stay grounded and respectful despite his stellar achievements. His parents have instilled in him simple values which have shaped him to be the person he is today. He could have reacted to his critics after winning the

World Championship. Instead, he admitted that he wasn't the best player in the world and had miles to go before he reached Magnus Carlsen's achievements, which he hoped to match. This has only endeared him more to the chess fraternity. Gukesh is a shining example that chess is a gentleman's game. In his own words, 'My mother urges me to be a good human being above anything else.'

Special
Chess Moves

Special chess moves let you make different types of movement or capture which are not possible by standard movements on the chessboard. Although there are not many special chess moves, it is essential that a chess player possesses a knowledge of them to play better chess. These three special moves are castling, promoting a pawn and capturing *en passant*.

- **CASTLING**
  Castling is the only move in chess by which a player can move two pieces on the chessboard at the same time instead of one. These two pieces are the king and the rook. Castling is also an important chess move because it helps you keep your king safe and protect him as well as develop a rook quickly. When castling

is allowed, one can move the king two squares to the side of the chessboard, then take it from the side you are castling and place the rook on the square that the king jumps over. When you move your king to the side that is closer to the edge of the board, it is called castling kingside or 'castling short'. When you perform the same action on the other side, it is called queenside or 'castling long'.

♟ **PAWN PROMOTION**

Pawn promotion is probably the only special move that all chess beginners know about, although there might be some confusion as to how this exactly works. In pawn promotion, a pawn becomes any other piece except a king when it reaches the farthest rank from where it had been placed. Pawn promotion becomes particularly crucial in a chess game, especially during endgames.

♟ **EN PASSANT CAPTURE**

The en passant capture is a rule in chess that allows pawns on the fifth for white and fourth rank for black to capture another pawn that has just gone past it in a single move. It is the sole capture in chess where the capturing piece does not land on the same square as the piece it is capturing.

Gukesh has shared that his mother keeps reminding him how important values and morals are in life. She shares inspirational stories from the Indian epics and insightful quotes on life with Gukesh that help him become a better person who is kind, considerate and empathetic. Her message always echoes in his ears whenever he is travelling and away from his mother – in life, success is incomplete if one is not kind and humble.

However, kindness and humility do not mean that you stop being aggressive in chess. Gukesh insists that one needs to fight for every inch at this level to win games. It is imperative that he stays alert, focused and competitive from the beginning to the end of his match as even a momentary lapse of reason can undo years of hard work and planning. He acknowledges the role of chess in shaping his life.

'Chess has taught me perseverance, patience and the importance of staying in the moment,' Gukesh said.

Gukesh's simplicity and humility comes through when he spoke of the support and sacrifice of his parents.

Grandmaster Kevin Goh was the head of the organizing committee of the World Chess Championship held in Singapore. He was really impressed with Gukesh, and lauded him with the following message: 'I finally managed to catch a word with this young gentleman, and like the well brought up lad he is, he expressed his thanks to our team for organizing the match. Also highlighted that the refreshments in his rest room were great. Never mind the chess skills, Gukesh represents his family, his country and the chess world really well with his sincerity, immaculate manners and composed demeanour. I am looking forward to see him reach even more peaks!'

'My parents have given up a lot in their own careers to see me succeed,' Gukesh said. 'My family has played a huge role in my journey. I'm incredibly thankful for their care and sacrifices. I continue to learn from them every day.'

Gukesh's father recalls having to sleep with his son in the airports as they could not afford a hotel during some of their chess journeys. Having seen it all from being financially secure to struggling for the fulfilment of their son's dream and now without any sort of financial worries, this great family has retained its humility, which is inspiring for everyone. Gukesh is also keen to inspire youngsters playing chess to realize their dreams, just like he had been inspired and mentored by Viswanathan Anand. He has revealed that he wants to inspire youngsters playing chess with not just his success but also with his discipline and dedication towards chess. He admits that this feels like a huge responsibility as he has to work harder now in order to set the perfect example for the younger generation. But there is also a playful side to him. Eighteen-year-olds are not expected to be serious all the time after all. This playfulness was apparent on Gukesh's Instagram post soon after his World Championship triumph. He posed with a funny sign that said, 'I know I am pretty, but please do not touch me.' This was in reference to the increasing number of fans who all wanted a piece of the world champion and desired to pose for selfies with him. The post soon went viral, garnering over two lakh likes in a short span of time. Gukesh's sense of humour to celebrate his success added to his popularity on social media as his increasing fanbase felt even more easily connected to him now. No wonder Gukesh's victory has inspired a global chess community. But it remains to be seen if he can become the king of chess in the future.

Before the World Championship, Gukesh participated in the Candidates Tournament which started on 4 April 2024. However, he was considered an underdog by the pundits. But after round five had concluded, everyone was in for a surprise as Gukesh was tied for first place. In the seventh round, he

Hypermodernism

Hypermodernism entered international chess in the 1920s as a new school of thought. The main thought is to control the centre of the chessboard with minor pieces instead of just occupying it with pawns. The application and theories of the talented chessmen of the era further ensured the progress of hypermodernism in chess, and the players included the likes of masters like Aron Nimzowitsch, Efim Bogolyubov, Richard Reti and Ernst Grünfeld. Several popular chess openings were also devised during this period, such as the Indian defences, the Benoni and the Grünfeld. But the most hypermodern of all chess openings is probably Alekhine's Defence, named after Alexander Alekhine, the fourth world chess champion who reigned from 1927 to 1935. The main idea of Alekhine's Defence is to invite the player playing in white to advance his central pawns and then attack the crowded centre.

Alexander Alekhine won the title again in 1937 and held on to it until his death in 1946. He is the only world champion in chess to pass away while holding on to his world championship title.

lost to Grandmaster Alireza Firouzja. This was a wake-up call for Gukesh in the tournament and by round 11, he had still not regained his share of the first place among the many heavyweights. In round 12 and 13, he surged to the top position again after two consecutive victories over Grandmaster Nijat Abasov, and he also won the rematch against Alireza Firouzja.

Thanks to his win against Firouzja, Gukesh was in first place when the final round of the Candidates began. But the lead was a slim one as he was only half a point ahead of the three chessmen who were the pre-tournament favourites to win the Candidates Tournament: American grandmasters Fabiano Caruana and Hikaru Nakamura and Russian grandmaster Ian Nepomniachtchi, who was the defending champion having won two of the previous Candidates tournaments. The four grandmasters were pitted against each other to decide the champion of the Candidates Tournament as Gukesh faced Nakamura and Caruana played Nepomniachtchi. A win for Gukesh against Nakamura would ensure that he won the tournament while he would be eliminated if he lost. Gukesh managed a draw against Nakamura. In the meantime, the game between Fabiano Caruana and Ian Nepomniachtchi also ended in a draw, making Gukesh the winner of the Candidates Tournament and also the official world championship challenger to Ding Liren.

The King's Gambit

In 1851, a famous chess match known as the 'Immortal Game' was played between German chess master Adolf Anderssen and Baltic German chess master Lionel Kieseritzky. This was a casual chess game. It is to be noted that the world chess championships had not yet begun then. Anderssen defeated Kieseritzky in this amazing game despite losing his rooks and queen to his opponent. The tactic used by Anderssen to win the game was named the king's gambit, a complicated tactic which became immensely popular in chess. In an unusual series of moves, Anderssen sealed his victory by sacrificing all his major pieces and developing a mating attack with the minor pieces that remained. The Immortal Game is one of the most famous attacking games in the history of chess and is considered important because it is the shining example of romantic play with several fantastic sacrifices and an amazing checkmating pattern. Despite ending up on the losing side, Kieseritzky was impressed with his opponent's brilliant performance.

8

THE TRAINING REGIMEN

A book cannot by itself teach how to play. It can only serve as a guide, and the rest must be learned by experience.
– José Capablanca
***Chess Fundamentals* (Published in 1921)**

Gukesh Dommaraju's rise to become world chess champion involved a lot of meticulous preparation, including an intense training routine. This training regimen included yoga, a detailed opening preparation and great focus on attacking strategies and calculation.

Yoga is a part of Gukesh's daily routine and plays a major role in enhancing his mental clarity and focus during high-pressure chess matches against strong opponents. Thanks to a daily dose of yoga, he has developed the ability of remaining calm under pressure and has improved his powers of concentration. During big tournaments, these abilities allow for optimum performances, as these skills make the difference when opponents are equally matched. Yoga also helps Gukesh maintain the right harmonious balance between his mind and body to face the growing demands of competitive chess. Gukesh has been spotted doing a bit of meditation before matches and sometimes even during his matches. Meditation, breathing exercises and yoga can do wonders for emotional stability and help a sportsperson not to burn out and withstand the pressure in their respective sport. Several chess players employ goal-based meditation and specific breathing techniques to focus on their chess matches. Gukesh also likes reading books on fitness and mental health. He read and liked a book written by his tennis idol Novak Djokovic, *Serve to Win,* which is based on a gluten-free fitness plan. One of his favourite books is *A Shot at History* by ace Indian shooter Abhinav Bindra. Gukesh also loves reading sports autobiographies as they really motivate him. He is the proud owner of the autobiographies of sports superstars like Sachin Tendulkar, Pete Sampras, Andre Agassi and Rafael Nadal to name a few. Gukesh's favourite books on chess include *Under the Surface* by the Slovak author and chess grandmaster Jan Markos and *Practical Chess Beauty* by Israeli chess player and author Yochanan Afek.

Cool Facts about Hot **Chess Moves**

- The longest chess game that is theoretically possible consists of as many as 5,949 moves.
- The number of possibilities of a knight's tour on the chessboard exceeds 122 million.
- The new pawn move, where pawns were allowed to move or advance two squares on their first move instead of one square, was first introduced in Spain in 1280 CE.

- America's Foundation for Chess states that there are 169,518,829,100,544,000,000,000,000,000 (approximately 1.70x10^29) ways to play the first ten moves of a game of chess.

- After one move each in chess, there are 400 different possible positions. There are 72,084 different possible positions after two moves each. There are over nine million different possible positions after three moves each and more than 318 billion different possible positions after four moves each. The number of distinct forty-move games in chess is far greater than the number of electrons in the observable universe. The number of electrons we have spotted so far is approximately 10^79, while the number of unique chess games is 10^120.

- From the starting position in chess, there are eight different ways to mate in two moves and 355 different ways to mate in three moves.

- Rookies are players in their first year of professional chess and have been named after the rook in chess. Rooks are normally the last pieces to be moved into action on the chessboard and the same applies for rookies in tournaments.

- In chess, there are over a thousand different openings.

Chess sets usually have thirty-two pieces to make moves with. But the popularity of chess has led to the inclusion of two extra queens making it thirty-four pieces. The two spare queens can be used in pawn promotion.

- The term 'gambit' is a chess term that means a 'sacrifice for advantage'.

- The term 'zugzwang' in chess describes a situation where a player would prefer not to move at all when it's his turn to make a move as doing so would worsen his present situation on the chessboard. A chess player who is forced to make a move in this tough spot is said to be 'in zugzwang'.

With so much passion for the sport, it's natural that Gukesh's chess regimen is extraordinary. The opening preparation of Gukesh is detailed and innovative. The introduction of fresh ideas in his chess openings haves been a characteristic feature of his play over the years, such as the move 6...Ng-e7, which highlights his ability to outfox his opponents by thinking outside the box. With so much depth and strategy in his arsenal in terms of openings, Gukesh has a slight edge over his much-fancied rivals and can wrest control and advantage of the game from the initial stage with a strong opening. His strength is not just knowing about the several moves or storing them in his memory to be deployed as per the occasion. It is his ability to understand the characteristic principles and the application of such moves and adapting them according to the different situations he faces during the game. Practising attack and calculation to improve his chess game is also a key feature of Gukesh's training regimen. His chess play features superlative attacking and calculation skills that he has taken years to nurture and master. His aggressive style makes his opponents go on the defensive and his uncanny ability to calculate long variations and predict probable outcomes displays his deep understanding of chess.

> The lethal combination of attack and calculation makes Gukesh a formidable opponent who can change the course of a game with a single, well-calculated move.

Gukesh's room is a modest, newly added suite on the first floor of the Dommaraju family house. The location is Korattur, Chennai. His space has a work chair, a table with a chessboard, shelves that boast of several trophies and books on chess openings and sports biographies. The room has a wash basin, a door that leads to a bathroom and a messy bed partly concealed by a curtain. This is where Gukesh spends the majority of his time when he is not touring. On a normal day, he likes to get eight hours of sleep. He loves playing physical sports, but has to stick to tennis as he doesn't have friends to play with because of his busy schedule. To keep fit, he works out at a gym in his spare time. But most of his time is spent on chess with Vishnu Prasanna, his trainer, who lives close by. Training also includes discussions about life in general and the desires, worries and hopes that are an integral part of life. These discussions sometimes take hours and are important to free the mind from pent-up thoughts and feelings.

It was a shift in routine and lifestyle that actually helped Gukesh turn the tide in his favour. Gukesh did not have a good show at the Grand Swiss tournament. After returning home to Chennai, he thought that qualification for the Candidates Tournament was impossible after this dismal performance and decided to take a break from chess. Little did he realize then that this break would do him a lot of good and this decision, coupled with a few others, would actually help him qualify for the Candidates 2024. A break was much needed for Gukesh, as he had been playing non-stop chess and needed to recharge his batteries by taking his mind off chess for a while. Earlier, he used to sleep late at night and wake up in the afternoon. Now he changed his lifestyle to wake up early in the morning to play tennis. Gukesh was seventeen years old when this change of routine took place. Gukesh's father was surprised when Gukesh woke up every day at 5.30 a.m. to play tennis. Breakfast was followed by other work and he would hit the bed religiously by 9–9.30 p.m. This routine continued for a week and then the invitations for the London Chess Classic and the Chennai event arrived. Gukesh was in two minds initially, but decided to take part in both events just to see how it went. He had a serious chat with his coach Grandmaster Vishnu Prasanna and it was decided that he would not think about the Candidates Tournament at all. Instead, he would just focus on playing good chess and nothing else. The results, although not instantaneous, did materialize slowly. Gukesh managed to qualify for the Candidates, surprising everyone. The rest, as they say, is history.

Vishnu Prasanna recalled his student's hunger to win and love for chess even during the early days. He said Gukesh used to play almost 230 games in a year, which is quite a lot. When he was not playing chess, he would train, even if he was travelling. But as he grew older, he cut down on his hours of playing and replaced them with ten to twelve hours of practice every day, including building his stamina and physical fitness. That barely left time for anything else in his life. The challenge for both Gukesh and Vishnu Prasanna was to keep distractions away, and when you are a teenager, there are plenty on offer. So for Gukesh, to devote so much time to chess, indicates his sheer passion and dedication towards the sport. 'Everybody wants Gukesh's outcome, but they do not want his lifestyle or habits,' Vishnu Prasanna stated, in reference to the countless parents who came to him and requested him to make their kids into a world champion like Gukesh, without wanting to work so hard. Unfortunately, there are no easy roads to succeed in life, especially in sports.

D. Gukesh versus Arjun Erigaisi at the Tata Steel Chess Tournament, 2023

HOW TO BECOME A CHESS GRANDMASTER

Becoming a grandmaster is the ultimate dream for a professional chess player. However, out of the millions of chess players across the globe, only about fifteen hundred chess players or more have attained this great title. The summit is difficult to scale but not impossible.

The World Chess Federation is known as FIDE, or the Fédération Internationale des Échecs. FIDE grants chess players appropriate titles based on their achievements and the title of grandmaster is the supreme title of recognition that is officially bestowed on a professional chess player. The basis of attaining the titles held by a chess player depends on them achieving a specific Elo rating, as well as achieving norms. These norms are awarded to a player on the basis of his performance in a norm tournament.

There are three basic steps that one should take to become a chess grandmaster.

1. **Participate in Tournaments**
   Unless skills are tested, one can never gauge how good one is. It helps to participate in local tournaments and learn from your losses to become a better player. Participating in tournaments, however small, gives you the basic ideas of time management, puts your skills to the test, helps you understand competition

and helps you gain experience to emerge as a stronger player in the next tournament. It also shows you whether you are good enough to compete at a global level.

2. **Score Three Norms**
   A chess player has to score three norms en route to becoming a grandmaster. To score these norms, he has to play in norm tournaments, which have at least three grandmasters participating from different countries. A norm tournament has nine rounds and a time control that is 120 minutes at least. A norm tournament also has an international arbiter present for the rulings to be made during the tournament. Last but not the least, the chess player who is looking to score a norm must have a rating of 2600 Elo for that tournament.

3. **Achieve a 2500 FIDE Rating**
   If achieving the three norms by playing in norm tournaments wasn't tough enough, a chess player also has to cross the 2500 FIDE rating to receive the title of grandmaster.
   In case you think being a chess grandmaster isn't really your cup of tea, here are some of the other FIDE titles and their respective requirements on offer.

Men's FIDE Titles	Requirements
Candidate Master (CM)	Elo Rating of 2200
FIDE Master (FM)	Elo Rating of 2300
International Master (IM)	3 Norms and An Elo Rating of 2400
Grandmaster (GM)	3 Norms and Elo Rating of 2500

Women's FIDE Titles	Requirements
Woman Candidate Master (WCM)	Elo Rating of 2000
Woman FIDE Master (WFM)	Elo Rating of 2100
Woman International Master (WIM)	Elo Rating of 2200
Woman Grandmaster (WGM)	Elo Rating of 2300

9

MENTAL TOUGHNESS

Some people see life as a game of chess, while others prefer to see it as a game of cricket; but the longer I live, the more I think of it as a game of Consequences.
– Craig Brown
(English critic and author)

Even though chess was invented in India and has a rich legacy in the land, cricket is the No. 1 sport here. Every child who grows up in India is passionate about cricket, their era and their favourite players. Gukesh is a self-confessed cricket fan as well, and his favourite cricketer is none other than the legendary former Indian captain M.S. Dhoni (MSD).

There are two reasons for this adulation. The first is because MSD led the Indian cricket team to two famous World Cup victories, one each in the ODI and T20 format in 2011 and 2007 respectively. In 2013, India also won the Champions trophy under Dhoni's leadership. The second reason is that Gukesh was born and brought up in Chennai, and is naturally a big fan of the IPL team Chennai Super Kings (CSK). Because of his association with CSK, Dhoni is a cult figure in Chennai and has been nicknamed Thala. This is no surprise as Dhoni has steered CSK to an astonishing five IPL titles. Gukesh has acknowledged that M.S. Dhoni was his childhood idol and a great source of inspiration. Gukesh has learnt the ability to perform under intense pressure from the great cricketer and has adapted the same mindset in his chess career.

'I admire M.S. Dhoni for how he handles himself under pressure,' Gukesh said. 'He is always calm and focused, no matter the situation. That is something I try to bring to my own game as well.'

MSD had said in an interview that he does not think too much about the outcome of the game, and this is what helps him ward off the monkey called pressure off his back. Does Gukesh feel the same way? Sometimes, things become easier if you just focus on the game and give your best instead of thinking about losing or winning. Gukesh also received the best training in mental conditioning from Dhoni's trusted mental coach, the one and only Paddy Upton. The South African mental conditioning coach has had a great love affair with India. He began his journey with the victorious Indian cricket team in the 2011 ODI World Cup. In the 2024 Paris Olympics, Paddy Upton worked with the Indian Men's Hockey team to help them win a bronze medal, their first podium finish in over four decades. In 2024 came the moment with Upton contributing to his historic World Cup championship win with Gukesh that he himself called the cherry on the cake. However, this cake has been baking for several years now and there's a lot of honey and chocolate on the cake as well. Paddy Upton has also been a part of ten IPL tournaments. However, his contribution to Indian sport is immense and praiseworthy. Gukesh acknowledged the important role played by Upton in his victory, saying that his South African mentor had helped him develop as a player and was responsible for his mental toughness.

After Gukesh won the Candidates, he felt the need for a mental trainer to help with his overall mental conditioning. He requested Sandeep Singhal of WestBridge Captial to recommend a mental trainer, and the latter put Gukesh in touch with Paddy Upton, who seemed to be the right fit, having worked with so many high-performance sportspersons like M.S. Dhoni, Virat Kohli, Rohit Sharma, P.V. Sindhu and Lakshya Sen. When Paddy Upton first spoke to Gukesh's sponsor Sandeep Singhal, he was unsure about working with a seventeen-year-old chess player. But after he met Gukesh and spoke with him, Upton realized he was in the presence of someone special and agreed to coach him. He explained later that he was hesitant to coach Gukesh initially because of two reasons. The first was that he did not know anything about chess and second, he did not coach sportspersons who were too young because they lacked the desired emotional maturity, the ability to self-reflect and have self-awareness of their own thinking, talent and emotions. But Paddy Upton was impressed early on in his first conversation with Gukesh when he understood that the young player was mature beyond his years and that his ability and self-awareness levels were supreme. Gukesh realized rightly that in a world championship it was not only about the skillset or talent in chess as one also had to weather a lot of emotional and mental issues to come up on top. Once Paddy was on board, his vast experience gave Gukesh the impetus he needed, and he treasures the numerous conversations he had with Upton, whose greatest credit is that he refined Gukesh's approach to the game. Upton's coaching philosophy focuses on detailed preparation, and Gukesh developed a robust mental framework under his trainer so that he could compete at the highest level and emerge triumphant. No wonder Paddy Upton considers Gukesh's achievement as the highlight of his coaching career.

'If you want to succeed, you need to study the whole book,' Paddy Upton revealed famously after Gukesh's historic victory. 'Gukesh has done exactly that. He is well prepared not only in terms of his game but also how he manages his sleep, downtime and overall mindset,' Upton explained after the conclusion of the World Chess Championship.

'Paddy has been a huge, huge support for me in the last six months,' Gukesh declared after his famous win. 'Although he is not part of my chess team, he has been a very, very important person in this journey. One of the critical aspects we worked on was managing the uncertainty around my opponent's form and approach. Paddy doesn't understand chess deeply, but he understands sport and the psychology behind it.'

Gukesh in 2023

Gukesh in 2024

Paddy Upton feels that Gukesh is a thorough professional who had all the bases covered as he prepared for the World Championship. He termed it as a gold standard preparation as Gukesh had looked at every single aspect that was likely to affect his performance right from attention to detail about his eating habits, exercise, sleeping, strategy meets with his team, tactical methods for the opening and the endgame, the mental aspect of the game, socializing with people as well as his downtime, when much-needed rest was required between the heavy-duty games which took a toll on both mind and body. Upton revealed that Gukesh paid great attention to his recovery time as well, ensuring that he got enough time for recovery and rest, but not too much as that could affect his performance in the next game. This-gold standard preparation by Gukesh ensured that there were no regrets going into the World Championship as all the boxes had been ticked. This is not as easy as it reads or looks as several athletes or teams either under-prioritize or over-prioritize some crucial aspect of training which they regret later. Neither cutting corners nor over-preparation is good. Upton felt that Gukesh managed all his aspects so efficiently and professionally that regardless of whether he won or lost, he would have no regrets. But normally when you leave no stone unturned, you win, and that's what Gukesh did.

Playing Chess Online

The twentieth century witnessed the dominance of technology in all sectors, and it moved forward at breakneck speed. Chess was impacted as well by technological advancements like the development of databases, highly intelligent chess engines and other modern techniques that took the game forward by leaps and bounds. These technological changes and advancements marked the end of the 'Romantic Era' in chess to begin what is known as the 'Online Era'. It slowly became sort of a trend to play chess online, and this was convenient too as there was no physical partner needed to play chess anymore. During the COVID days, when human beings learnt the true meaning of isolation and solitude, online chess surged in demand and popularity. Gaming platforms like the MPL or Mobile Premier League surfaced like hot cakes for hungry chessmen as online chess spread like a virus globally. Now people could easily play chess with someone anywhere in the world and choose from different playing levels by just downloading a mobile gaming app. They could also win real cash rewards sitting at home.

In a game like chess that could stretch for as long as six to seven hours, it drains out all your energies and creative juices. So the ability to stay completely focused is the difference between a win and a loss. In team sports like cricket, football, basketball and hockey, players get the opportunity to switch up and down easily and rectify their errors later. But chess offers no luxury as it's a relentless battle with no respite and barely any time to recharge your batteries during a game. One bad move and you're finished, unlike a second innings in cricket and a second half in football where you can make a comeback.

Mental skills play a key role in chess as they enable a player to recognize their strengths and weaknesses. Strong mental skills make a chess player more self-assured by making him more stable. There is no overestimation or underestimation of one's opponent, which makes him approach the game with an even mind. Sharp mental skills ensure strengthening of resolve and the rapidity of moves and decisions in a chess match, which is important in the rapid style where one has to think fast. Last but not the least, there are no disturbing feelings in the mind.

> Mental toughness is important for all sports, and especially chess. In a mental game like chess, which is not a physical or contact sport, like football or even cricket, the demand of every moment is complete focus and total concentration.

When Paddy Upton coached Gukesh on his mental skills, he found an eager student who already had a self-awareness that was beyond his years. Upton equated this quality to that of Jacques Kallis, famous South African cricket all-rounder and one of the greats of the game. He said that just like Kallis, Gukesh was an introvert by nature and both had the same personalities. Both Gukesh and Kallis were capable of staying in their own bubble, unaffected by whatever was happening around them. But Upton said that Gukesh had this special quality where he shone brilliantly in big moments. Gukesh has that big-match temperament, which brings out his best performance in important games and tournaments. Upton equated this capability of Gukesh in chess to that of Virat Kohli in cricket, who, despite the recent slump in form, scored 76 runs in the finals of the T20 Cricket World Cup 2024, when it mattered the most.

The Benefits of **Playing Chess**

Chess is one of the most popular and loved games in the world that offers many benefits. Cognitive skills such as memory, problem-solving and planning are greatly enhanced by playing chess. Chess might also reduce the symptoms of some brain conditions. However, this is not entirely conclusive. But there's no denying that chess is indeed good for mental health, as it stimulates the intellectual faculties of the brain to good effect. Here are some benefits:

- By playing chess, one develops the unique ability of viewing things from the other person's perspective. The next moves of the opponent are anticipated beforehand by an experienced and skilled chess player. For this prediction to be made in a chess game, a player must develop the skill or ability to know what the opponent is thinking and gaining an insight into his perspective. That makes it easy for them to deduce what action the opponent is most likely to take. Behavioural scientists have termed this skill or ability the 'theory of the mind'. This helps a person become more empathetic and build healthy social relationships as well. Studies have revealed that children who play and practise chess develop this unique perspective-taking ability early on in life.

- Chess boosts creativity and planning skills. Chess is characterized by silent contemplation as players ponder over their next move. Thoughtful contemplation and planning is thus enhanced, which is also one of the cognitive health benefits of playing chess. A cognitive functioning test with pegs and beads was conducted between two groups, one that played chess and one that didn't. It was revealed that the group playing chess displayed much better planning skills than the group that did not play chess. People in the chess-playing group also took more time to make their decisions than the other group.

- Chess players naturally have strong memory skills as the game requires that they memorize the various combinations of moves, strategies and possible outcomes. Chess players also have to keep several things stored in their memory like the various opening, middlegame and endgame strategies and combinations. Chess players with a better auditory memory, which is what they have learned through hearing, also perform better than their counterparts with limited memory power. Memory also helps chess players recall visual patterns on chessboards and relating them with complex chess situations they have studied before in games of chess or chess theory.

- Playing chess helps people enter a flow state, which is a sense of total involvement in something that is deeply enriching and rewarding. It's like entering a zone where everything else is inconsequential or irrelevant, including the awareness of anything else except the game of chess, which is being played because of the intense focus that is demanded. The scientific explanation for this state is that the theta waves are heightened in EEG's or electroencephalograms taken in a state of flow. During intense chess matches, studies have revealed the same high levels of theta waves in brain scans of experienced chess players.

- Counsellors and therapists often recommend chess to their clients. Some also play chess with them to build better therapeutic relationships and increase self-awareness and confidence. Thus, chess is also used to make therapy more effective. Chess also protects old people from dementia by keeping their mind active because of the mental flexibility that is used to play chess.

- Chess can also improve attention-deficit/ hyperactivity disorder (ADHD) symptoms as a 2016 study has revealed. A hundred schoolchildren affected with ADHD were exposed to regular chess playing. The participants were greatly benefited as there was a 41 per cent decrease in inattentiveness and hyper activity after the course of this unique multifaceted treatment.

'I've been very impressed with his maturity and his thinking, specifically in his self-awareness of what he's thinking about, and what's going on for him. He definitely has a self-awareness that is beyond his years. Obviously, he's a chess genius. But he's got an amazing self-awareness and ability to self-regulate,' Upton said, praising Gukesh. Upton also said that the big boys step up and deliver when the pressure is the highest. He cited the example of the 2011 World Cup final when guys like M.S. Dhoni and Gautam Gambhir performed when it mattered the most to take the team home. Gukesh is driven the same way, he said, to discover his best form and perform his best when the stakes are the highest.

But how did a professional like Paddy Upton, who had no previous experience of coaching a chess professional, adapt to this challenging task? After all, he had only worked with professionals in sports boasting of a strong physical component like cricket, hockey and rugby. Upton is of the view, however, that the mental demands across all sports at the highest level are similar and constant, and his process does not change with the sport. But each sport has its own unique demands, according to the South African. For example, a midfielder in football processes more external information about his opponents than his other counterparts, while the focus of a golfer is totally internal as he is reliant on mostly body awareness and his mindset to take a shot. But in chess, the mental side plays the most crucial role as speed and stamina coupled with physical dominance and skill is not enough to dominate your opponent like a Messi or a Ronaldo. But chess has a physical and mental exhaustion of a different kind as it stretches to as long as fourteen games in a tournament. Upton tried a different approach with Gukesh to counter this chess exhaustion. He laid stress on Gukesh's overall well-being and had long discussions with him on several aspects of his life outside chess as well as his approach to the game. Upton also encouraged Gukesh to dabble in sports other than chess, like tennis, to refresh him mentally and physically. The idea was to create a balance so that Gukesh could perform his best without getting exhausted. Upton also worked on Gukesh's thought process during matches to learn how he approached the various phases of the game, what he thought when he was ahead or behind in the game and how he prepares for the next game after a win or a loss. Upton thinks that the mindset is important to address for Gukesh to recover from setbacks quickly and keep his focus for the next match to bounce back.

Apart from working on Gukesh's mental conditioning, Paddy Upton also helped out by planning his workout sessions in a detailed manner and aided his physical fitness. Upton gave Gukesh some great tips that helped him get sound sleep during the tournament. Due to the demands of time, all the sessions between Upton and Gukesh were of a virtual nature, with Zoom as the preferred medium. Each session lasted for an hour to an hour and a half for five months before the World Championship. These sessions were more conversational than instructional and the sole aim was for Gukesh to understand his thoughts,

The Cosmic Connection of **Chess**

The chessboard on which the game of chess is played is made up of sixty-four squares. The board is a representation of the world or the universe, which is considered a manifestation of the primeval cosmic man and the supreme spirit. The chessboard is also the field on which the game of chess is played and the square grade of sixty-four squares is basically 8x8. Eight was symbolic of intrinsic harmony, excellence and stability in ancient India. Eight is also the number of the primary and intermediate cardinal directions, the parts of a kingdom, the parts of a court of law, as well as the parts of the human body. 8x8 is the best of excellence which keeps rising in time.

emotions and life better so that he could manage them more effectively and be prepared for the gruelling challenge of the tournament. Most of it focused on discussion and reflection even though Upton gave Gukesh an activity or exercise to try on his own from time to time. But the key was to get Gukesh mentally prepared and have an idea when to step back as the mental side also demanded breaks and recovery like the physical side. Otherwise, fatigue sets in and to avoid burnout, downtime and mental recovery are absolutely important. Upton cited the example of an athlete who would not hit the gym for hours every day before a big event as he had to unwind.

Similarly, chess players needed time away from the sport to reset their mental batteries so that their mental resources are not exhausted. In a nutshell, Upton considerably improved Gukesh's mental resilience, pressure-management skills and recovery strategies in only a period of six months. Another star Paddy Upton compared Gukesh to was the Indian cricketing legend Rahul Dravid. He said Gukesh's humility reminded him of Dravid. That's high praise indeed!

Max Warmerdam versus Gukesh Dommaraju

10

THE HUNGER TO WIN

Without the element of enjoyment,
it is not worth trying to excel at anything.
– Magnus Carlsen
(Norwegian chess grandmaster and World No. 1 player)

Gukesh is a fierce competitor who has the hunger to win in chess as well as in life. This was demonstrated at a private event in September 2024, after Gukesh had made waves by securing a double gold at the Olympiad. Gukesh was present at this event with grandmasters R. Praggnanandhaa, R. Vaishali and Srinath Narayanan. Instead of chess, the four grandmasters were paired against each other in a fun contest. The test was against a punch measurement device, similar to the ones present in arcades. Gukesh was not happy with his score after he had landed a punch. The organizers gave him a couple of more tries till Gukesh was satisfied. This illustrates Gukesh's dedication and his fierce apetite to win even if the game in question is a fun event. The teenager is a competitive and hardworking individual with a unique and perfect blend of both the traits, who also learns from his mistakes to become better. His desire to win has made him take difficult decisions in life without batting an eyelid, where most would have taken ages to arrive at a conclusive decision. He was so confident about his prowess in chess that he decided to drop out of elementary school, a move even his parents were sceptical about despite their unconditional support for him. After Gukesh took the inconceivable step, at least by Indian standards, and dropped out of school in the fourth standard to pursue chess, many were surprised. In 2015, Gukesh scored his first big victory at the Asian School Chess Championships Under-9. In 2017, Gukesh's father displayed his support further when he quit his job so he could travel with Gukesh to his chess tournaments. This was a tough call as Gukesh had no sponsors and his family had to manage all his expenses especially travel. They were also reliant on Gukesh's prize money winnings and crowdfunding so that all his expenses could be met. So the call taken by Gukesh's father was a tough one but also inevitable as someone needed to travel with the young Gukesh.

Gukesh's mother had to take care of the financial burden of running the family, and she did a wonderful job. In 2018, Gukesh won the Under-12 World Youth Chess Championships and a record five gold medals at the Asian Youth Chess Championships to announce his arrival in the world of chess.

Viswanathan Anand had spotted Gukesh's talent as early as 2017. So when Anand founded the WestBridge Anand Chess Academy (WACA) in 2020, Gukesh was part of the first batch. A year earlier, however, the twelve-year-old Gukesh became the then second-youngest grandmaster in the history of chess. The hunger for victory was evident. In 2022, Gukesh won the gold medal at the 44th Chess Olympiad. Soon after, he became the youngest player to beat World No. 1 Magnus Carlsen. In August 2023, Gukesh surged ahead of Viswanathan Anand, his idol and mentor, to become India's No. 1 chess player. He also became the youngest player to cross the 2750 rating in chess. As of now, only thirty-two chess players have a FIDE rating above 2700.

Gukesh's intense desire to win can be attributed more to his tenacity than his skills. In the encounter with Ding in the World Championship, for example, several other players in Gukesh's situation would have played for a draw and then retired to their room to prepare for the tie-breaks that would decide the outcome of the match. Even Ding was playing for a draw as he fancied his chances in the tie-breaks. But Gukesh kept prodding and pushing and looking for a way to win instead. Gukesh was not the kind of player who would be satisfied with easy draws. So much like a Karpov or a Carlsen, Gukesh squeezed his opponent to the point of exhaustion so that he committed one of the most amateurish blunders of the game.

Cool Facts about

Chess Grandmasters

- According to research, chess grandmasters have high IQs. The top-ranked grandmasters are in possession of the highest IQs. A chess player who reaches a maximum rating of 2000 is expected to have an average IQ. Chess players with a rating of 2600 and above are experienced grandmasters who usually have an IQ of 160 and above.

- In 1920, an eight-year-old chess player named Samuel Reshevsky defeated several chess masters at once in France.

- In 1960, an American chess master called George Koltanowski played a total of fifty-six games simultaneously. But he played them all blindfolded, and had only ten seconds per move at his disposal. Koltanowski won fifty games and drew six games. When these games were concluded, George Koltanowski was able to recall every move for every game from memory.

- The world record for a simultaneous chess exhibition was set in 2011, according to Guinness, by Iranian chess grandmaster Ehsan Ghaem-Maghami. He faced as many as 614 chess players in a span of twenty-five hours in a marathon chess match. The Iranian grandmaster won 590 games, or 96 per cent of his games, with sixteen draws and eight losses. As he walked up and down the aisles to make his moves during this marathon contest, he walked approximately 34 miles.

- The only grandmaster to win the World Championship in all the three formats in the knockout, tournament and match formats is Viswanathan Anand from India.

- At least twenty-three chess players have become grandmasters before they turned fifteen years old. Bobby Fischer was the youngest grandmaster for as long as thirty-three years as he became the youngest grandmaster in 1958 aged just fifteen and a half. In 1991, Judit Polgár beat Fischer's record as she became a grandmaster at fifteen years and four months. However, several players have received the title of grandmaster at surprisingly young ages.

- The present record for the youngest grandmaster in chess is held by Abhimanyu Mishra of the United States who became a grandmaster aged twelve years, four months and twenty-five days.

- The youngest woman to become a grandmaster in chess is Hou Yifan of China, who did so at the age of fourteen years and six months. Only thirty women have achieved the full grandmaster title (not WGM).

- All the women who have earned the grandmaster title in chess are still alive. At the age of thirty-seven, Judit Polgár is on top of the women's ratings list. The current women's world champion Chinese Hou Yifan is close behind.

- The most common initials of chess grandmasters are 'A.K.' As many as thirty international grandmasters share these initials like Anatoly Karpov, Alexander Khalifman and Alexandra Kosteniuk. Anton Korobov of Ukraine is the current highest-rated player with these initials being the 116th ranked player in the world, while Russian Anatoly Karpov is the most famous.

The victory over Ding and winning the title of world champion gave Gukesh entry into what Garry Kasparov had once called the 'most exclusive club' in the world. Including Gukesh, there have been only eighteen members in this exclusive club in the past 138 years. This is the exclusive club of the world champions of chess. Before FIDE was established and chess was brought under a regulated body globally, the World Championships held between 1886 and 1946 saw the emergence of five great champions from five different countries. They were Wilhelm Steinitz from Austria, Emanuel Lasker from Germany, José Raúl Capablanca from Cuba, Alexander Alekhine from France and Max Euwe from the Netherlands. The period of 1946 to 2007 saw the Russians dominate the game of chess, except in 1972 when Bobby Fischer of the USA burst onto the scene and won the world title. But after a brief reign, Fischer faded away into oblivion, with the Russians asserting their supremacy again. The Russian rule ended in 2007 when the great Indian grandmaster Viswanathan Anand won the title and held on to it till 2013 to begin the great Indian revolution in chess. In 2013, Magnus Carlsen defeated Anand to become the new world chess champion. Then in 2024, Gukesh not only became the second world champion from India after his idol Anand, but he also made India the only country in the world other than the erstwhile USSR to have produced more than one chess world champion. That is another reason for Indians to celebrate this triumph.

India has become a major global chess powerhouse thanks to a plethora of young talents who have burst onto the chess scene. Apart from Gukesh, another young star is nineteen-year-old Rameshbabu Praggnanandhaa (R. Praggnanandhaa), a chess prodigy from Chennai. He is known as Pragg to fans and players in the chess circuit.

> Pragg has called for a more robust financial backing for chess in India and highlighted the need for corporates to step forward and support the sport.

Coming back to Gukesh, he has acknowledged that Magnus Carlsen still remains the best player in the world, and the fact that he would have liked at a crack at Carlsen is obvious. Magnus Carlsen decided not to defend his world championship any more in 2021. However, he's not the first grandmaster who has stepped down as world champion without being actually defeated for the title. In 1975, the American grandmaster Bobby Fischer refused to defend his world title against a young and dangerous challenger named Anatoly Karpov because FIDE refused to meet his three non-negotiable demands. So Fischer refused to defend the title he had won in 1972 after beating Boris Spassky, and Anatoly Karpov became the world champion. This had led to a lot of questions about the young Karpov's credibility back then and the world of chess had mostly refused to acknowledge Karpov as a true champion as he had not actually defeated the previous king. However, Karpov had silenced all his critics by becoming one of the greatest chess players in history in the days to come. Anatoly Karpov dominated chess for as long as ten years before another young Russian challenger dethroned him from the pole position.

A Lot to **Pragg About**

- Rameshbabu Praggnanandhaa or Pragg started playing chess when he was five years old. At the age of ten years, ten months and nineteen days, he became the youngest international chess master. When he was twelve, Pragg became the second-youngest grandmaster in the world.

- Praggnanandhaa is also the first Indian to qualify for the prestigious Candidates Tournament since 2016.

- He's the only second Indian to reach FIDE World Cup final. Pragg reached the final by beating World No. 3 Fabiano Caruana in the tie-breaker of the FIDE World Cup semi-finals.

- In 2022, Pragg stunned the chess world by defeating the Norwegian World Champion Magnus Carlsen at the Airthings Masters. He is only the third Indian who has managed to beat Carlsen and also the youngest player ever to do so.

- In 2023, Praggnanandhaa and his sister, twenty-two-year-old Rameshbabu Vaishali (R. Vaishali) became the first-ever brother and sister to receive grandmaster titles in the history of chess.

- In February 2025, Praggnanandhaa won the Tata Steel Masters chess event in Wijk Aan Zee, Netherlands, after rallying from behind to defeat world champion D. Gukesh 2–1 in the tie-breaker.

Today's formidable fourteen at the Tata Steel Chess Tournament 2025

11

THE UNDISPUTED LEADER OF THE NEW GENERATION

Tactics is knowing what to do when there is something to do. Strategy is knowing what to do when there is nothing to do.

– Savielly Tartakower
(Polish/French chess grandmaster)

Writing in her column in the *New in Chess* magazine, Grandmaster Judit Polgár has called Gukesh a dynamic and fearless chess player. She has also called him the 'undisputed leader of the new generation'. It is easy to see why Judit Polgár has labelled Gukesh thus. If we compare Gukesh with the rising Indian stars of chess, we can see that he has a style that is most attacking. He is also the player who is most keen to get a decisive game among all the players globally. However, his playing style is more suited to classical chess as of now, rather than rapid chess, as he likes to take his time to make a move. When we compare Gukesh's playing style to that of Pragg or Arjun Erigaisi or even someone like Nihal Sarin, we see that Gukesh is the one who is most likely to make the craziest of moves and lines and is also the most volatile among them in terms of results. Gukesh has displayed in the past that he can play with a combination of the skills of Magnus Carlsen, Anatoly Karpov and Garry Kasparov, and that is what makes him such a dangerous opponent.

When it comes to time controls, Arjun Erigaisi is most well-rounded. However, he does not play as much offensive-oriented chess as Gukesh, although he is more offensive than Pragg. Erigaisi's strengths on the chessboard are his rapid moves and perceiving and detecting threats from his opponent. Pragg probably is the most solid chess player among all the Indian rising stars and is blessed with great intuitive skills to figure out engine lines. Pragg is also a stable player with flashes of genius like he displayed in his victory against Magnus Carlsen. In comparison, Nihal Sarin's playing style is a bit strange. He has great experience in online chess, but despite his great attacking skills online and being the fastest among all the four young Indian players, he is more of a conservative player. If his performance is any indicator, he does not look likely to join the other three in the exclusive 2750 club.

Gukesh has strong points, but his weaknesses are also evident when compared to his peers. Although he wins many matches, he also loses more than the other players at his level. Gukesh is more of a positional player who is not good when under time pressure, and in quicker time, controls where moves have to be taken quickly. In rapid chess, for example, he can lose from winning positions, making a mess of things sometimes. Pragg has had lesser defeats in recent teams because he is the hardest to beat among all four. But Gukesh has a fearless tactical style, which is why he is considered ahead of his peers. Although his openings are not planned deeply, he has this uncanny knack of creating a variety of openings and innovates as he plays. He does not always play what you call the best computer move, but sometimes, his moves are deep and surprising, which gives his opponent a tough time. In a defensive situation as well, Gukesh can come up with surprisingly good moves. His achievements appear extraordinary when one considers that he is just

THE EVOLUTION OF CHESS AS A ROYAL GAME IN EUROPE

During the fifteenth century, chess evolved as a 'royal game' when kings like Henry I, Henry II, Ivan IV, Alphonso X and Philips II were introduced to chess and began playing the game religiously. But even before it was deemed a royal game, chess was already popular in Europe. In the thirteenth century, alarmed at its popularity over other things, King Louis IX enforced a ban on chess in the land as he thought it was a boring and useless game that distracted people from praying to God. But not even kings could stop the sport from being played as the love for chess was so deeply rooted that it blossomed again to become the game of 'kings and nobles' now. In India, chess was always considered the game of kings ever since its inception during the reign of the Gupta dynasty to its patronage during Mughal rule. But chess in ancient India was used to communicate war strategies as well as entertain purposes. Cut to the present, where chess still serves multi-functions like recreation, competitive sport and the development of the brain as well as cognitive skills. The game of kings has not diminished in popularity even today but has become more universal and is played by people from all age groups and classes.

eighteen years old. Grandmasters who are twice his age have not been able to reach the levels he has reached:

- Crossing the 2750 Elo rating mark in 2022.
- Bagging two golds at the 2024 Chess Olympiad and scoring nine out of ten.
- Victory at the 2024 Candidates Tournament to emerge as the youngest challenger to the world championship crown.
- Winning the World Championship trophy in 2024.

Cool and Collected

Chess Facts

- Some of the current names of the chess pieces reflect the origins of these names. For example, the rook is known as 'rukh' in the Persian language and means 'chariot'. Chariots were an integral part of ancient Indian warfare and were also incorporated as chess pieces.
- Pawns are the smallest pieces on the board and their role in chess is always undermined. However, in the earlier versions of the game like chaturanga, pawns symbolized

the infantry division of the army and were considered strategically important in chess.

- The most expensive chess set in the world is the Jewel Royale Chess Set, which is valued at over $9.8 million. It is made of gold, diamonds, sapphires, platinum and other precious stones.

- The Folding Chessboard was invented by an English priest who wanted to play chess desperately. This was in 1125, when priests were forbidden to play the game, and this priest came up with the novel idea of concealing the chessboard like a book to avoid detection. The folding chessboard looks like two books stacked on each other.

- Chess has inspired several variations, all of which have their own rules and regulations. Prominent among them are 3D chess, Fischer Random Chess or Chess 960 and Bughouse or team chess. In Fischer Random Chess, the starting positions of the back pieces are randomized, and this means that players have to be more reliant on their creative moves to win rather than memorized openings.

- Online chess platforms have become really popular in today's world and players from all across the world can now compete with each other by sitting at home. Sophisticated algorithms are used by these online chess platforms so that players of similar skill levels can be matched and clubbed against each other.

Gukesh has been inspired by many legends, and it all began with Viswanathan Anand. However, Anand is not only Gukesh's role model but also his mentor, as Vishy took all the talented young chessmen under his wing at his WestBridge Anand Chess Academy (WACA). Under the programme at WACA, which lasted from January 2021 to November 2022, Gukesh and the other Indian rising stars of chess were helped by Anand and big names like Artur Yusupov, a three-time World Championship candidate and Boris Gelfand, 2012 World Championship challenger. The aim of the programme was to help some of the boys break into the top 10 in the world of chess. But what Gukesh did was phenomenal.

In 2005, Gukesh hadn't even been born when the great Garry Kasparov retired from chess. Yet, the influence the Russian great has had on Gukesh is undeniably deep and effective. Gukesh's home library boasts of collections of several classical games of the past, including those of Kasparov, as he is heavily influenced by the tactics and strategies of the former Russian world champion. Kasparov's unique style included his panache for hunting kings, handling of knights and calculating combinations that lasted for dozens of moves. A part of Gukesh's play is reminiscient of the play of the great man. For example, he also uses his knights to create magic on the chessboard. 'Aggressive knights' is a theme that is synonymous with Gukesh in the chess circuit.

Carlsen is considered the master of prophylaxis and restriction of the opponent. But where style of play is concerned, Carlsen and Gukesh are like night and day as Carlsen likes iron-clad control in the game, while Gukesh's style involves crazy positions with mind-boggling complications. Gukesh's coach Grandmaster Vishnu Prassana has revealed how Gukesh meticulously studied Carlsen's games, especially how the Norwegian master anticipates the moves and ideas of the opponent to nip them in the bud. This helped Gukesh become a better attacking player and use pinning for restriction. So he's learnt a lot from studying the moves and strategies of Carlsen as well. But Gukesh is the player that he is today by merging the lessons of Viswanathan Anand with Garry Kasparov's tactical vision and Magnus Carlsen's positional control. He is quite a sight as he uses his queen to force open the strongest of defences, opens lines of attack, thanks to his favourite pawn breaks and plays on both flanks simultaneously to tear apart the defences of the opponent. However, there have been several legends in the history of chess other than the ones who have inspired Gukesh. Here's hoping that Gukesh Dommaraju finds a place in this exclusive list in the future.

Top 10 Best Players
in Chess History

Before we dive into the exclusive list of the top 10 best players in the history of chess, it would be a crime not to mention three legends, who narrowly missed the mark to feature in the exclusive chess club of the best players ever.

PAUL MORPHY

Even though American Paul Morphy narrowly missed the mark to be featured on this list, he is considered the strongest chess player of the 1850s and one of the best in the nineteenth century. He finds a place in Grandmaster Bobby Fischer's list as one of the ten greatest chess players of all time. Although there was no world championship during Morphy's playing days, and this is the main reason why he doesn't find a place in the top 10, Morphy is widely acknowledged as the unofficial world champion, as he was way ahead of his competitors. After his triumph in the 1857 American Chess Congress, Morphy travelled to Europe a year later where he won every match he played against the world's best players. Morphy's contribution to chess included sacrifices, development, attack strategies and accuracy in moves. His Opera Game is one of the most famous games and is studied to date.

TIGRAN PETROSIAN

The second genius to miss out on the list is Armenian-Soviet Grandmaster Tigran Petrosian, known in chess circles as 'Iron Tigran'. He was a four-time Soviet champion and the world champion from 1963 to 1969. In 1962, Tigran Petrosian was undefeated for the entire year before becoming the world champion. Petrosian was one of the first chess players to have a universal style and was famous for his defensive abilities and exchange sacrifices.

VISWANATHAN ANAND

Vishy or Viswanathan Anand is the strongest Indian grandmaster of all time and is responsible for the revival of chess in India. He was crowned the fifteenth world champion after defeating Vladimir Kramnik in 2008. This five-time world champion from India was dethroned by Magnus Carlsen in 2013. Despite his great contributions to chess, Anand failed to make the Top 10 narrowly.

Here's the list of top 10 players in chess history.

10. ALEXANDER ALEKHINE

Tenth on the list is Russian/French Grandmaster Alexander Alekhine, who was the fourth official world champion. Alekhine's USP was that he was an exceptional player with all-round abilities and had a special flair for combinational play in complex positions. His contribution to the chess world was that rules and principles can be broken with the application of detailed analysis of specific and unique positions. Famed for his tactical prowess, Alexander Alekhine's contribution to chess theory is also remarkable. He authored more than twenty books on chess, and two of them are regarded among the best chess books of all time. Alekhine defeated José Raúl Capablanca in 1927 to become the world champion against all odds as he had never won against Capablanca before. Alekhine defended his world championship title twice in 1929 and 1934, defeating the challenger, Grandmaster Efim Bogoljubov both times. In 1935, he lost the title to Grandmaster Max Euwe and won the title back from him two years later. Alekhine died in 1946 as the world champion and is the only champion to have ever done so.

9. MIKHAIL TAL

Latvian-Soviet chess player Mikhail Tal is No. 9 on the list and was also known as the 'Magician from Riga'. Tal was the eighth official world champion and defeated his namesake Mikhail Botvinnik in 1960 to become world champion. Tal was only twenty-three and a half years old and the youngest world champion then. Later, this record was broken by Garry Kasparov and Magnus Carlsen, and more recently by Gukesh Dommaraju. Mikhail Tal was famous for his unique attacking style which bamboozled his opponents. Tal has inspired attacking chess players for centuries and his book *The Life and Games of Mikhail Tal* is considered a chess classic and one of the greatest books on chess.

To quote the great Mikhail Tal himself, 'You must take your opponent into a deep dark forest where 2+2=5, and the path leading out is only wide enough for one.'

8. EMANUEL LASKER

The second official world champion, Emanuel Lasker, holds the eighth position. The German chess player beat the first official world champion Wilhelm Steinitz in 1894 and held the title for twenty-seven long years. His rule from 1894 to 1921 is the longest of any world champion to date, as he defended his title five times, beating serious contenders like Frank Marshall, Siegbert Tarrasch, David Janowsky and Carl Schlechter. He finally relinquished the title to José Raúl Capablanca in 1921. Lasker was not just a tactical giant but also used a psychological approach to chess to the effect that he deliberately played inferior moves sometimes to confuse his opponents. Some say that

Lasker influenced Albert Einstein in his thoughts and applications of the theory of relativity to physics. A famous letter Einstein wrote to Lasker in 1931 says, 'I cannot explain how your chess influenced my thinking, but it certainly did.'

7. VLADIMIR KRAMNIK

World champion from 2000 to 2007, Russian Grandmaster Vladimir Kramnik is in seventh place. The legendary Garry Kasparov was beaten by Kramnik for the World Championship title in 2000. Kramnik was tough to beat at his peak and was most famous for his endgame play and his impressive and workmanlike positional style. He played for over twenty-five years before finally retiring from chess in 2019.

6. MIKHAIL BOTVINNIK

Known as the 'father of the Soviet chess school', Mikhail Botvinnik was the sixth world champion and is also 6th on this list. Botvinnik was on top of his game for more than thirty years. His style featured strong logic and flexibility as well as methodical and strategic planning.

Botvinnik became world champion in 1948. In 1957, he was dethroned by Grandmaster Vasily Smyslov, but Botvinnik won the rematch a year later to reclaim the title. In those days, the world champion had the right to a rematch after losing the title. Tal defeated Botvinnik in 1960 for the title, but history repeated itself as Botvinnik won the rematch in 1961. In 1963, Petrosian ended Botvinnik's reign as world champion. The same year, Botvinnik started his chess school, becoming the teacher and mentor of three future world champions and chess legends: Anatoly Karpov, Garry Kasparov and Vladimir Kramnik.

5. ANATOLY KARPOV

Fifth on the list is the Russian grandmaster Anatoly Karpov who was the twelfth world champion and ruled from 1975 to 1985. Karpov was also the FIDE world champion from 1993 to 1999. Karpov had fantastic all-round abilities, but what set him apart was his brilliant prophylactic play, positional binds and a fantastic endgame technique. In 1984, Karpov played his first match with Garry Kasparov, and this began the famous Karpov vs Kasparov duels which transformed the chess world forever. Their record in world championship matches against each other stands thus: nineteen wins for Anatoly Karpov, twenty-one wins for Garry Kasparov and one hundred and four draws. No rivalry could get better than this one!

4. JOSÉ RAÚL CAPABLANCA

The third official world champion José Raúl Capablanca is fourth on this exclusive list. Considered by many to be the most talented player to play chess, he had the record of forty wins and twenty-three draws in tournaments from 1916 through 1924.

This was a superlative feat and Capablanca was unparalleled during this period of eight years remaining undefeated. In 1921, Capablanca became world champion by defeating Lasker. Sadly, Capablanca was at his peak during and between World War I and World War II. Capablanca's endgame was so superior that even in today's modern era of chess engines, it is tough to find loopholes in his endgame play.

3. BOBBY FISCHER

Bobby Fischer was the first and only American world champion in chess history. Chess is one area where the Americans failed to dominate the Russians. However, the eleventh official world champion is considered by many to be the most famous chess player in history.

In his brief period of sheer brilliance, Bobby Fischer won twenty consecutive games against top opposition from 1970 to 1971. This historic achievement might never be equalled in chess and features among the seven most amazing chess records. In 1972, Bobby Fischer and Boris Spassky locked horns in what was termed the 'Match of the Century'. This became one of the most famous chess games of all time and Fischer defeated Spassky to be crowned the world champion. Fischer's brief domination of the Soviet chess empire from 1970 to 1972 in the middle of the Cold War was not only a matter of national pride for Americans but also one of the greatest individual performances of all time.

Fischer had a unique, creative, original and distinct style. It involved both attack and defence, but with a crazy positional understanding.

2. MAGNUS CARLSEN

Magnus Carlsen is No. 2 on the list but has been the No. 1 ranked player in chess since 2011. He has dominated the scene since then. In 2009, the

Norwegian grandmaster became the youngest player in the history of chess to reach a rating of 2800. Carlsen was crowned the world champion when he defeated Viswanathan Anand in 2013. He was just twenty-two years old then.

In 2014, Carlsen reached the highest ever live rating of 2889. He is also the only chess player to win the world championship in all time controls in the standard, rapid and blitz categories. In 2019, he held all three of them simultaneously. Carlsen is famous for his versatile playing style and deep knowledge of the game. He is more of a universal player rather than specializing in particular openings or styles, but his endgame is particularly praiseworthy as he has won from impossible situations sometimes. His tenacity in longer games and the ability to remain calm under extreme pressure has earned him the nickname the 'Endgame Virtuoso'.

Many believe that Magnus Carlsen is the greatest chess player of all time, but the great man agrees with our list. He considers Garry Kasparov to be the best ever because of his twenty year reign as the world No. 1. But Carlsen also feels that age and time are both on his side. So we'll just have to wait and watch.

1. GARRY KASPAROV

Garry Kasparov is our Numero Uno on this list

simply because he dominated the world of chess for more than twenty years. A twenty-two-year-old Kasparov became the 13th world champion after dethroning Anatoly Karpov and held the title from 1985 to 2000. Kasparov's playing style features his aggressive moves and detailed opening preparation. His tactical skills and the use of sharp and complex lines made him a dreaded opponent. His intense focus, deep knowledge of the game and psychological approach were additional weapons to outfox his opponents. Garry Kasparov and Emanuel Lasker are the only two world champions who have defended their titles successfully as many as five times. Kasparov's golden rule ended in 2000 when he was defeated by Vladimir Kramnik. But Kasparov kept on playing the game and retired only in 2005. To his credit, he retired as the number one player in the world. Kasparov is still active in the world of chess and has trained greats like Magnus Carlsen and Hikaru Nakamura.

12

THE FANS OF THE PRODIGY

There is technology where you can watch the match live online and also on TV. If people understood the game, I'm sure we would have a lot of chess fans by now.

– Viswanathan Anand
(Indian chess grandmaster)

It's not surprising that Gukesh Dommaraju's victory at the world chess championships has increased his fan following considerably both in India and outside the country. The adulation for Gukesh is evident both by the huge crowds that had gathered to welcome him at Chennai airport and the buzz around the teenager on social media in the form of posts, videos and comments that celebrate his success. Among the ocean of posts, a small video clip has managed to capture the hearts of all viewers. This video displays the heart-warming interaction between Gukesh and one of his tiny fans. As part of the closing ceremony, fans were granted a chance to interact with the superstar. But it was his youngest fan who stole the show. A little girl from Singapore was seen walking up to Gukesh, holding something in her hands. The excited wide-eyed girl asks for Gukesh's autograph with a beaming smile. A humble Gukesh was speechless when the girl offered him a pillow to autograph. The unusual stuffed pillow is a special one as it has both the little girl's as well as Gukesh's face on it. Gukesh of course happily granted her request. You can catch this cute video on the Instagram page called 'Chess with Lokesh' and it has the apt caption that says 'Cutest fan, sweetest gift, greatest Gukesh'.

A game of nerves

> This connect that Gukesh has with young people could make him the idol of the next generation as well as popularize chess further.

Jump cut from Singapore to Gukesh's arrival at Chennai airport from Singapore to be mobbed by thousands of fans. In India, the fan frenzy is so great and the effort and commitment some fans display is so humongous that we suspect that they would have done rather well for themselves had they chosen a sport. Take, for example, the curious case of Rahul Kamble. Our man travelled almost 850 kilometres on cycle from Belgaum in Karnataka to Chennai in Tamil Nadu to see his chess idol Gukesh.

One suspects that very soon Karnataka will also jump in the fray along with Tamil Nadu and Andhra Pradesh to claim Gukesh as their son of the soil. Kamble explained his cycling action rather simply, 'I came here to meet Gukesh. He shook hands with me, and that moment was worth everything. I've been on the road cycling since November 25, supporting Gukesh. Along the way, I visited several chess academies. My dream is to take a photo with Gukesh and my cycle. From here, I plan to travel across Tamil Nadu.'

Kamble is a chess trainer at a private school in his hometown Belgaum, and his t-shirt proudly says 'D Gukesh' above the No. 64. We have no idea why the number is 64 and not something else. The banner on his cycle makes more sense as it proclaims 'All India Cycling Tour for Chess'. Season 2 – Belgaum to Chennai.' Whoever says there is no physical effort in chess should probably meet Rahul Kamble, whose journey ran parallel to Gukesh's successful world championship campaign. When Kamble's school management refused to grant him the permission to embark on his wild cycling adventure because they needed someone to teach chess to their students, Kamble quit his job to support his hero. He pedalled furiously to make his way up north to Goa and then travelled to Mumbai when the Candidates Tournament was in progress. After Gukesh won that, a superstitious friend advised Kamble to continue his cycling journey as it was bringing luck to Gukesh. An equally superstitious Kamble agreed, and Lady Luck continued to smile upon Gukesh. As ardent fans of Gukesh, we pray that Kamble gets a sponsor now and continues his cycling journey whenever Gukesh plays in 2025. Yes, we Indians are a superstitious lot for sure!

Celebrity Chess Fans Who **Didn't Make the Cut**

Thanks to the internet, chess has become a sport for the masses and the fact that you don't need an active partner to play the game anymore makes the sport more acceptable and interesting. From the common man to celebrities to world leaders, the passion for chess is common and infectious. We turn the spotlight on fifteen international celebrities who are unified in their common love for chess.

1. JIMMY CARTER

The thirty-ninth president of the United States, Jimmy Carter, was a passionate chess player. He even toyed with the idea of becoming a chess expert after the end of his presidential term. To make this dream a reality, Jimmy Carter purchased chess books as well as a computer chess programme. But he abandoned his dream when realization finally dawned upon him that he didn't possess a natural talent for chess.

2. ARNOLD SCHWARZENEGGER

Arnold Schwarzenegger's core philosophy in life is to merge physical strength with mental prowess to achieve greatness. That's what probably sparked his keen interest in chess, or it could be that he wanted to become a smarter actor. In his own words, 'There is nothing like chess to keep the brain smart and give it a workout.' Arnie often posts pictures where he's seen playing chess in the gym of all places and sometimes with his fans.

We have no doubt that Arnold Schwarzenegger intimidates his opponents psychologically by flexing those biceps as he makes a move and growls, 'I'll be back!' after a defeat. Wonder if the Terminator has a good endgame!

3. MADONNA

Who's that girl? Well, it's none other than Madonna playing chess. The iconic pop star is an avid chess player who has played as many as 19,000 games on the Internet Chess Club. Madonna apparently takes the game more seriously and made the effort to be taught by the Scottish chess champion Alan Norris. You can spot her playing chess in her music video 'The Power of Good-Bye,' although 'This Used to Be My Playground' would have been a better choice. Madonna also plays chess with her children to help them think critically and develop their problem-solving skills.

4. JAY-Z

The famous rapper Shawn Carter, aka Jay-Z, picked up chess from his father and promoted the game in the United States by sponsoring tournaments. He once said, 'I'm the Bobby Fischer of rap.'

5. DAVID LETTERMAN

The famous late-night talk show host is known for his legendary wit and sense of humour and his interaction with celebrities. But did you know that Letterman is also a great chess player? In 1989, he actually played a game against then World Champion Garry Kasparov. Surprise, surprise! It actually ended in a draw. Knowing Kasparov, he wouldn't have settled for anything less than a win. Maybe Letterman promised him a hot seat on the show.

6. STEPHEN FRY

Actor, writer and intellectual Stephen Fry loves playing chess. In 1988, his documentary Grandmaster Clash, about the Chess olympiad held in Thessaloniki, Greece, that year, was widely praised for its accurate depiction of a chess player's professional life.

7. BILL GATES

The man who co-founded Microsoft is also a chess lover. One moment he will treasure all his life was playing a televised exhibition game against Magnus Carlsen in 2014. Even though poor Bill lost in just nine moves, the game was instrumental to grab the eyeballs of the entire chess community and popularized the sport further.

8. ELON MUSK

Elon Musk was part of his school chess team.

Later on in life, he decided that he would be better off founding landmark companies like Tesla, Space X and Neuralink rather than playing chess professionally.

Come to think of it, Musk would have probably succeeded in chess as well. He often gives his hot take on chess philosophy on online platforms.

9. PETER THIEL

The co-founder of PayPal and Palantir Technologies, Peter Thiel was also an early investor in Facebook (read Meta). Thiel is also credited with shaping Silicon Valley with his investment acumen and innovative plans. Thiel was an active tournament player in his youth and finished ahead of Hikaru Nakamura in the US Open. Even though he chose business over chess, he holds the title of National Master and currently has a FIDE rating of 2199.

10. DEMIS HASSABIS

Artificial intelligence researcher Demis Hassabis has done it all, from being a child chess prodigy who competed with Judit Polgár to becoming a Nobel laureate. The British CEO of DeepMind Technologies has also revolutionized chess, thanks to his contribution to AlphaZero. He was given the honour of making the ceremonial first move at two world championships. The first was the 2018 match between Carlsen and Caruana and the second was between Gukesh and Ding Liren in 2024.

11. RICHARD BRANSON

British businessman and adventurer Richard Branson is famous for heading the Virgin Group. But he is also fond of chess and can be seen playing chess in his free time wherever he is. Branson has also taught chess to his children.

12. WOODY HARRELSON

Hollywood actor Woody Harrelson, who is famous for his films like *Zombieland* and *Natural Born Killers,* is an avid chess player. Because of his enthusiasm for the game, Harrelson has been given the honour of making ceremonial first moves in many world chess championship matches. Such as the ceremonial first move he made in the 2016 World Championship match in New York, between Magnus Carlsen and Sergey Karjakin. His ceremonial opening move at the 2018 championship match in London became famous for its light-hearted moment. Making the move for Magnus Carlsen, Woody Harrelson knocked down Fabiano Caruana's king.

13. MO SALAH

We now move on to footballers who play chess, and Mo Salah might be the best footballer to play chess in current form. The Egyptian star is addicted to chess and regularly plays online. What's impressive is that Salah has a rating of 1400. Mo Salah has also expressed his wish to play with World No. 1 Magnus Carlsen. But that event looks as unlikely as Egypt winning the FIFA World Cup.

14. PEP GUARDIOLA

One of football's most famous and innovative managers, Pep Guardiola rose to fame as the coach of Barcelona and Bayern Munich. But he became a legend with Manchester City. A grand football strategist, Pep confesses that he has learnt a lot from stress strategy and says that there are a lot of things that are common in football and chess.

Pep has highlighted the importance of the centre in both sports for example.

15. YUZVENDRA CHAHAL

Indian cricketer Yuzvendra Chahal is the only player to represent India in both cricket and chess. Yuzi represented his country in chess at the World Youth Chess Championship but gave up the game later as he struggled to find a sponsor. He was smart enough to choose cricket where he has made a name for himself as one of the finest leg-spinners of his era. Yuzi has credited the game of chess as being instrumental to teach him the importance of patience over the years. He certainly needs to be patient the way he's constantly in and out of the Indian cricket team despite being a top performer.

While Gukesh can boast of an enviable fan base globally, there is also a mutual admiration society with the movie stars he himself idolizes. India is a country which treats its film stars like gods and goddesses, and the fans of the South Indian film industry are arguably the most passionate. The Tamil film industry is one of the leading film industries of India, and Rajinikanth is considered the superstar of the Tamil film industry and a legend of Indian cinema. Gukesh loves his dose of cinema whenever he gets the time. Gukesh's family has been fans of Rajinikanth for three generations, and Gukesh's father was named Rajinikanth after the superstar by his grandfather, who was a huge fan.

Gukesh met superstar Rajinikanth after his victory on being invited to his residence along with his parents. Rajinikanth was clad in a black kurta and grey lungi as he posed for pictures with Gukesh and his parents. He gave a shawl to Gukesh and a very thoughtful book, *Autobiography of a Yogi*, the 1946 spiritual classic by Paramahansa Yogananda. Gukesh wrote later on his social handle, 'Thanks Superstar @rajinikanth sir for your warm wishes and inviting, spending time and sharing your wisdom with us (folded hands emoji).'

But Rajinikanth is not Gukesh's favourite actor. That honour is reserved for Sivakarthikeyan, and Gukesh also met him after his victory. For the uninitiated, Sivakarthikeyan garnered a lot of praise for his portrayal of Ashoka Chakra recipient Major Mukul Anand in Rajkumar Periasamy's war film *Amaran*. Sivakarthikeyan gave Gukesh a luxury watch, which he placed on the wrist of his young champion fan, and this brought tears of joy to Gukesh's eyes. We are unsure if the gift of a watch is an indication to Gukesh to speed up his game as well as his ratings in rapid chess by his favourite movie star. Sivakarthikeyan took time off from his busy schedule to come and meet Gukesh at his Chennai residence, and this is what made this meeting so special and emotional. Clad in a light T-shirt and black trousers, Sivakarthikeyan also fed Gukesh a piece from a customized chess-themed cake. An emotional Gukesh wrote later, 'Had a great time with @Siva_Kartikeyan sir and he was kind enough to spend time with me and my family despite his busy schedule and enjoyed a lot!'

Get used to it, Gukesh. Everyone in India will be kind enough to spend time with you – the youngest chess champion of the world.

13

A GLOBAL BRAND AMBASSADOR?

In chess, as in life, play the best move.
– Irving Chernev
(Chess player and author)

Gukesh's victory at the World Championship has served as an inspiration for the Indian as well as the global chess community that chess can be a career option instead of just a sport. Younger players have been inspired after seeing the eighteen-year-old become such a formidable force in chess. The young chess players in Tier 2 towns across India have gained the most motivation as chess surges in popularity in even the remote corners of the country. The fact that Gukesh serves a role model for these youngsters is a good sign as it is also hoped that they will imbibe his hard work, resilience, work ethics, dedication and, most of all, his humility. Cricket legend Sachin Tendulkar has rightly stated that Gukesh had opened a world of endless possibilities.

'Following in Vishy's footsteps, you're now guiding the next wave of Indian chess prodigies,' Sachin Tendulkar wrote on X. Gukesh will be pleased with what Abhinav Bindra, former Olympic champion in shooting, had to say on him as Bindra's book was a major inspiration during his younger days.

'Your brilliance, determination and grace under pressure have made the entire nation proud. You've not just won a title but inspired a generation to dream big. Wishing you even greater success ahead!' Bindra wrote about Gukesh. Congratulations also arrived from the Indian prime minister and president after Gukesh's victory.

'Historic and exemplary! Congratulations to Gukesh D on his remarkable accomplishment. This is the result of his unparalleled talent, hard work and unwavering determination,' Prime Minister Shri Narendra Modi wrote on X. 'His triumph has not only etched his name in the annals of chess history but has also inspired millions of young minds to dream big and pursue excellence. My best wishes for his future endeavours.'

President Droupadi Murmu said that Gukesh's win stamps the authority of India as a chess powerhouse. Several sports stars, celebrities and politicians have commended Gukesh for bringing back the world title to India. The buzz doing the circles right now is the possibility of Gukesh dethroning Magnus Carlsen as the global grandmaster of chess in the world. If Gukesh continues his superlative performance in chess, and there is no reason why he shouldn't do so after becoming the world champion, brand strategists are hopeful about the sport being endorsed in Tier 2 cities as well as rural pockets of the country.

Indian rising stars of chess are drawing the big brands. Adani and Indian Oil Corporation Ltd (IOCL) are sponsors of R. Praggnanandhaa, or Pragg, Vidit Gujrathi has Ambit, Persistent and Oil and Natural Gas Corporation Limited (ONGC) backing him; the Murugappa Group supports Aravindh Chithambaram and Nihal Sarin is endorsed by Akshayakalpa. Arjun Erigaisi has been snapped up by Quantbox in a historic five-year sponsorship deal of $1.5 million (more than ₹12 crore). The Pravaha Foundation gives ₹2 crore as funds over a period of two years to support six Indian women chess players, including the likes of Savitha Shri Baskar and Vantika Agrawal. These sponsorships are vital for a chess player, and many a talented sportsperson has dropped out of the sport because of a lack of funds or sponsorship. Right now Gukesh is a brand ambassador of RBL Bank.

Magnus Carlsen has long been the undisputed king of chess as well as a global ambassador for chess. He endorses top brands like Mastercard, Puma, Anichess, Chess.com and a few betting companies. Viswanathan Anand has endorsed brands such as Horlicks, AMD, Parle Milk Shakti, Air India, Samsung, Amul, NIIT, Vodafone and Crocin. He has recently been roped in by the internet chess server Chess.com as their brand ambassador. In 2023, American grandmaster Fabiano Caruana was roped in by Chessify as a brand ambassador. Chessify is a platform which aims to level the playing field in chess by making advanced technologies accessible to players from all levels. FIDE has recognized Chessify as the No. 1 cloud service for chess engine

FIDE CHESS RATINGS (as of February 2025)					
INDIA (ACTIVE PLAYERS – MEN)					
Rank	**Name**	**Title**	**Rating**	**Games**	**Birth Year**
1	Arjun Erigaisi	G	2801	9	2003
2	D Gukesh	G	2777	14	2006
3	Viswanathan Anand	G	2750	0	1969
4	R Praggnanandhaa	G	2741	1	2005
5	Aravindh Chithambaram	G	2729	2	1999
6	Vidit Gujrathi	G	2721	7	1994
7	Pentala Harikrishna	G	2695	0	1986
8	Nihal Sarin	G	2687	18	2004
9	Raunak Sadhwani	G	2666	9	2005
10	Murali Karthikeyan	G	2651	18	1999

analysis, which is valued by professionals and amateurs alike. It is expected that Gukesh's popularity and World Championship victory has accelerated the boom already present in chess in India. Any brand looking beyond cricket, the most popular sport in India, is now expected to be looking at chess for their brand needs, according to experts who also feel that the endorsement market for chess in India is really expected to open up. This is because of Gukesh's appeal and reach to target an estimated fifty million chess fans in India, including youth, which is a staggering number and a mouth-watering prospect for any established brand, both national and international.

FIDE CHESS RATINGS (as of February 2025)					
INDIA (ACTIVE PLAYERS – WOMEN)					
Rank	**Name**	**Title**	**Rating**	**Games**	**Birth Year**
1	Koneru Humpy	GM	2523	0	1987
2	Divya Deshmukh	M	2490	0	2005
3	Harika Dronavalli	GM	2489	0	1991
4	Vaishali Rameshbabu	GM	2476	0	2001
5	Vantika Agrawal	IM	2411	1	2002
6	Tania Sachdev	IM	2396	0	1986
7	P.V. Nandhidhaa	WGM	2380	9	1996
8	Rakshitta Ravi	WGM	2365	9	2005
9	Bhakti Kulkarni	IM	2357	9	1992
10	Padmini Rout	IM	2356	18	1994

Currently, brand strategists are of the opinion that chess grandmasters could collaborate with brands like tech, AI or educational firms to create strategic business partnerships. But the battle will be really won if brands of all varieties rope in Indian grandmasters, just like cricketers endorse everything from food products to cars and bikes. Chess champions are actually perfect brand ambassadors for banks, financial services companies, insurance companies, IT, children's products and products that are for the brain. This is because a chess player in India is cost effective and comes much cheaper for a brand than a cricketer. Hungarian chess player Susan Polgar, winner of four women's world championships and five Olympic gold medals in chess, has endorsed brands like a bank and an insurance company in her native land.

'Generally, investments are linked to strategies and computers to their computing power, both of which chess players signify,' Polgar explained. 'Companies are aware of this aspect. They use a chess piece or the board as part of their advertisement even if they do not use a chess champion as their brand ambassador,' she said. The brand-endorsement scene is much lucrative for European chess players than their Indian counterparts. Norwegian Magnus Carlsen, for example, signed endorsement deals with Nordic Semiconductor, Arctic Securities, Simonsen Vogtwiig and VG, a Norwegian newspaper, when he was still a title challenger to Viswanathan Anand. The world's top chess players may be charging no less than $1,00,000 for endorsing a brand. That is still less than what Indian cricketers charge in India for endorsing a product. Many chess players from India, especially those not from financially strong backgrounds, have had to quit playing chess for the lack of finances or a sponsor.

Susan Polgar has an interesting suggestion to make the game of chess more spectator friendly. Polgar suggests changing the format of chess slightly to transform it into a spectator sport. She also advised the chess players to be more media friendly and savvy so that their marketability goes up considerably. Chess has witnessed a glorious resurgence in 2024, and the money in the sport is also on the rise, along with the excitement. There is an increase in tournament prize money, sponsorships, streaming and online chess platforms like Chess.com and Twitch, to name a few. The World Chess Championship can transform the financial status of the champion remarkably, as Gukesh discovered after his win being richer by an astronomical ₹11.5 crore. Some chess players also increase their revenues by becoming major influencers and creating content for YouTube and Twitch to increase their fan base even more. Legends like Magnus Carlsen and relatively new stars like Alireza Firouzja have demonstrated how to turn a creative passion into a rewarding business model, as their love for chess has also led to increased inflow in their bank accounts.

Let's take a look at the highest grossers in chess in 2024. This is, however, reflective of their earnings in 2023 from tournament wins only, because sponsorship money deals are often confidential. Hence, earnings from other sources such as streaming, endorsements and business projects do not find a place in this list below.

The Elite Top 15

Richest Chess Players in the World

Here are the top 15 richest players in chess – the real movers and shakers. The fact that two women chess players and two young male Indian grandmasters have found a place on this list makes it even more special.

1. **DING LIREN**
   Despite being dethroned by Gukesh, the Chinese player Ding Liren sits at the top of the list. After his uncharacteristic blunder and disappointing loss, Ding Liren will seek some consolation that he amassed a staggering

$12,28,200 in tournament prize money alone in 2023. Liren's massive earnings indicate his phenomenal talent as well as the huge financial opportunities that have opened up in international chess.

2. IAN NEPOMNIACHTCHI

Russian chess Grandmaster Ian Nepomniachtchi earned $12,26,825 in 2023 through tournament wins and did not miss out by much to Ding Liren for the top spot. His sharp tactical style makes him perform well at tournaments, and his performance at the World Chess Championship was also noteworthy.

3. MAGNUS CARLSEN

The Norwegian superstar is third on the list by earning $7,05,155 in 2023 from his tournament performances. He would have probably made the top of the list if he had played in all the major tournaments. But he did not participate in the World Chess Championship. He'd certainly top the list if all sources of total revenue are taken into account.

4. FABIANO CARUANA

American Grandmaster Fabiano Caruana

is fourth on the list of richest chess players from tournament earnings having grossed $6,38,372 in 2023. Two of his secrets in winning tournaments are his strategic planning and great preparation for tournaments.

5. **WESLEY SO**

   Filipino-American chess Grandmaster Wesley So had a great tournament run in 2023 by becoming richer by $3,94,542. Wesley So has been one of the most consistent performers in top-flight tournaments and always seeks to improve his game after each tournament.

6. **JU WENJUN**

   The women's world champion Ju Wenjun is the first lady on this exclusive list with earnings of $3,54,581 in 2023. She earned this staggering prize money on account of her dominance in various tournaments. This highlights both Ju's dedication and talent to make her the perfect role model for all young and aspiring female chess players in the world.

7. **HIKARU NAKAMURA**

   American chess Grandmaster Hikaru Nakamura is one of the wealthiest chess players, thanks to his popularity in online streaming on platforms like YouTube and Twitch. But he's only seventh on this list, having raked in $2,84,527 from tournament earnings in 2023. However, there is life after chess for Nakamura, and he's sorted with his retirement plans.

8. **MAXIME VACHIER-LAGRAVE**
French Grandmaster Maxime Vachier-Lagrave was a consistent performer in 2023 tournaments, earning $2,82,854, showing that he is one of the best players in the global circuit. He has a sharp and tactical style of play that makes him stand out and grab the eighth place.

9. **LEI TINGJIE**
The second woman on this exclusive list of rich people in ninth place is Chinese grandmaster Lei Tingjie, who is one of the most popular faces in women's chess. Lei made $2,57,171 in 2023 from her tournament earnings and is reputed for her fighting spirit and strong positional play.

10. **NODIRBEK ABDUSATTOROV**
Uzbek teen prodigy Nodirbek Abdusattorov is tenth on the list and earned $1,90,173 in 2023 in tournament prize money, displaying his tremendous and rapid growth as a chess player. He's an aggressive player with superlative tactical skills and could well become one of the top players in the near future.

11. ALIREZA FIROUZJA

Iranian-French grandmaster Alireza Firouzja is placed in eleventh position, thanks to the $1,84,402 he made from tournaments in 2023. He is characterized by his aggressive play and sharp, creative tactics to earn a great reputation in chess in a short span of time.

12. LEVON ARONIAN

Veteran American grandmaster Levon Aronian has proven that age is just a number even if you got plenty. The forty-two-year-old who became a grandmaster when he was only seventeen earned $1,82,175 from tournament wins in 2023. Old is definitely gold.

13. ANISH GIRI

Dutch chess grandmaster Anish Giri raked in prize money worth $1,69,799 in 2023. Known for his solid style of play and creative move strategies, Giri can also speak six languages like Russian, English, Dutch, Japanese, Nepali and German.

14. GUKESH DOMMARAJU

Our very own world champion Gukesh is fourteenth on the list having earned $1,42,555 in 2023. But the teen prodigy is sure to go up the charts in the list of 2025 as and when it is released after his exceptional win at the World Championship, where he has raked in the big moolah.

15. VIDIT GUJRATHI

Indian grandmaster Vidit Gujrathi earned $1,31,647 in 2023, displaying that he is a force to reckon with at the global stage. He has performed well in every major tournament and has also defeated Magnus Carlsen in a Pro Chess League match.

RANK	COUNTRY	AVERAGE	GMs	IMs	TOTAL TITLED
1	Russia	2739	256	549	2641
2	USA	2715	101	166	828
3	China	2705	48	39	181
4	India	2668	64	114	408
5	Ukraine	2663	93	209	589
6	Armenia	2652	44	29	132
7	Azerbaijan	2652	26	32	159
8	Hungary	2644	58	120	497
9	France	2638	50	118	465
10	Poland	2637	45	109	447

LIVING CHESS – A POPULAR SPECTATOR SPORT DURING MUGHAL RULE

The Mughals were probably the first to transform chess into a spectator sport in the truest sense of the term. But this is debatable as the Mughal reign in India began in the sixteenth century, and at the same time, Don John of Austria, former governor of the Spanish Netherlands, had 'living chess' being played in his court. The concept of living chess is rather interesting as it involved the use of humans as chess pieces and has been a legendary topic for decades. Written records of living chess have been found in books like *A History of Chess* (1972) by Jerzy Gizycki and Baruch H. Wood.

Tales of emperors such as Akbar (1542–1605) using captives or enemies to play living chess have been found in articles like 'Living Chess' in *Frank Leslie's Popular Monthly* (1883). It claims that Emperor Akbar played living chess on the pavement of the Pachisi court in his city of Fatehpur Sikri, where slave girls were used as chess pieces. This account has also been found in *Travels in India and Kashmir* (1853) by Erich Schönberg.

Akbar and his two viziers, or ministers, Abul Fazal and Byrber, supposedly played chess here with the living maidens serving as chess pieces. These slave girls were divided into two groups and distinguished by the colour

Two shatranj players in a detail from a Persian miniature painting of Bayasanghori Shahname, made in 1430

of their costumes. Four of them were dressed in black, four wore red, four yellow and four were clad in white. The emperor and his royal viziers were spared the effort of making moves on the chessboard by raising their imperial right hands, which could be used for something else now or just be relaxed. This was the game worthy of kings now as moves were dictated and the little feet of the slave girls moved from square to square to follow the orders issued. The winner who could checkmate the king was rewarded with a large prize that outshines the earnings of the top players in chess by a long shot. The living pawns, knights and castles were given to the winner along with other riches. It was certainly rewarding to play and win against the emperor.

Don John of Austria, on the other hand, had living chess played indoors and not outdoors like Emperor Akbar. The premise was a magnificent chamber, which was floored with a wide, square and chequered pavement made of black and white marble. Living chess was played here for the entertainment of his court, and the best players in the kingdom participated in these living, chess matches. The winner was rewarded handsomely, but the audience was lesser as compared to the Mughal living chess scene. The grand living-chess tournaments were made popular first by Akbar and then the legacy was carried forward by Jahangir and Shah Jahan. The grand matches saw the elite of Mughal society in full attendance, complete with royalty, courtiers and high-ranking officials, as opulence blended with strategy and entertainment. The gigantic chessboards were not just playing surfaces but the stages of a drama unfolding before fascinated eyes. Living actors played pawns, horses and elephants to add the element of theatre to an already fascinating and competitive game. Trained animals were also incorporated into living chess under Mughal rule, and they added a fascinating dimension to living chess. Trained elephants were the stars, as they gently moved on the giant chessboards under the guidance of their mahouts, drawing oohs and aahs from the gathered audience. Well-trained Arabian horses added to the spectacle as they moved across the chessboard regally, carrying their majestic knights. Trained birds like falcons and eagles were released into the air to hover above the giant chessboard. Although they played no active part in the game, these birds added the element of beauty and elegance to these living-chess matches to enthral the audience. The scale and grandeur of chess had never been higher and is testimony to the intelligence and sophistication of the Mughal elite. It's probably why chess has been termed 'the game of kings'. But this exercise also fostered cooperation, social interaction and diplomacy apart from sheer entertainment value in its carnivalesque atmosphere as courtiers could engage with their emperor on an equal footing. Chess also found a place in Mughal culture in art forms, literature and poetry, leaving behind a rich and everlasting Indian legacy.

14

THE WORLD IS MY FAMILY AND THE FAMILY IS MY WORLD

When the chess game is over, the king and the pawn go back in the same box.
– Italian proverb

Chess is more than a mere game as its highly strategic moves stimulate the mind greatly to have a significant impact on the overall development of a child who has an early introduction to the sport. The role of the parents in the development of a young chess player or prodigy who has displayed early signs of talent in chess is crucial. Parents play a vital role in kindling a child's passion for playing chess by providing both emotional and financial support. While the coach plays a key role, the involvement and support of the parents are a key catalyst for the young player to develop into a mature chess player. Gukesh wouldn't have tasted success without the support and sacrifice of his parents, who recognized the talent the prodigy possessed at an early age and took the difficult step of sacrificing their careers so that his dreams could be realized. One of the most emotional moments of the World Chess Championship was when an elated Gukesh ran outside to embrace his father after clinching the victory. This lovely bonding between a father and son touched the hearts of the fans worldwide. This was the culmination of years of hard work, sacrifice, dedication and love.

When Gukesh was asked later how he intended to spend the massive prize money of ₹11.5 crores, his answer reflected the humility we know him for. Gukesh replied that during the course of this journey, his family had drained all their financial resources so that he could chase his dreams. Chess is an expensive sport after all, and one cannot play the sport unless he or she is financially stable or backed by a sponsor. Despite his promising talent, Gukesh didn't have a sponsor during his struggling days. During periods of financial difficulty, his parents' friends had stepped forward to ensure that they never lacked funds, and Gukesh faced no obstacles in his chess journey. These were his parents' college friends, and Gukesh is very grateful to them. Gukesh said he was very happy that he could justify the faith shown in him by his parents and their close friends and that the sum he had earned as prize money would ensure the financial stability of his parents and their friends who had helped him when the going was tough. Gukesh reiterated that it meant a lot to him to have finally given peace of mind to his parents. Personally, he had never thought too much about money and had focused entirely on playing chess.

'But I understand money is a very important part of life. I will use this amazing gift that God has given us to improve ourselves and to help us reach our full potential,' Gukesh concluded. Such generosity, honesty, simplicity and gratefulness are rare in a world champion and especially in an eighteen-year-old. Gukesh's mother Padmakumari revealed that as a parent, one of the most difficult decisions was to withdraw Gukesh from schooling after the fourth grade. This was a crucial decision but also unconventional as education is considered the most important thing in India even if there is immense aptitude or potential for a sport displayed by a young person. But the times are changing in this country. At the same time it is also true that Gukesh's parents often doubted their actions, wondering if they had done the right thing, especially when Gukesh didn't perform well in tournaments.

In the end, it has proven to be the best decision ever made by Gukesh's parents for him. Another tough decision for Gukesh's father was to quit his job so he could travel with his young son for chess tournaments. Padma kumari had to bear the burden of being the sole breadwinner of the family and those were difficult days financially. Just like the queen on the chessboard, which is the most powerful piece, Gukesh's mother is a queen in her own right – the queen in Gukesh's chessboard called life. When Gukesh was playing his title match against Ding Liren in Singapore, his mother Padmakumari was at home in Chennai, India. But the enormity of the event made her too nervous to follow the match. So Padmakumari did not switch on her mobile or her computer that entire Thursday. She only received the news around 7 p.m., when Gukesh's aunt ran into the house excitedly to break the big news to her. Gukesh had been crowned the world champion. The trophy was coming home.

Gukesh, engrossed ...

How the Queen Replaced
The Minister

Chess officially arrived in Europe from Asia sometime during the tenth century. Other records show that when the Arabs conquered Persia as early as the seventh century, the game of chess spread slowly to the Middle East and then to Spain through the Moorish conquest and then to Byzantium. From Byzantium, chess spread to Italy first and then to other countries of Western Europe. Another theory suggests that the knights of the Crusade picked up the game in the Middle East to spread it across Western Europe. However, there was no queen on the chessboard then. Instead, the chess piece that stood next to the king on the chessboard was an advisor called the 'fer' or 'general' or 'minister' in the Middle Eastern and Persian versions of the game and a weak one at that being equipped with limited moves on the chessboard. This ministerial piece was transformed into the queen to reflect the royal family. However, the queen could move only one square at a time and that too diagonally. The queen gained both power and control in chess only in the fifteenth century thanks to the rise of powerful queens in Europe like Queen Isabella of Spain, Queen Elizabeth of England and Queen Katherine the Great of Russia. The queen officially became the most powerful piece on the chessboard.

Padmakumari was dumbstruck for a moment and then her emotions broke free like water gushing out of a dam. She couldn't believe initially what she heard, and when it finally registered, she cried for a full ten minutes. Soon it was time for Padmakumari to take the earliest flight to Singapore to join her son and husband. Even at the moment of success, which had been reached, after so much of struggle and sacrifice, Padmakumari did not forget anyone who made this journey easier like their other family members, including grandparents, sisters, in-laws and friends. She said she was thankful to each one of them.

'My parents had to make many lifestyle changes just for me to play tournaments. They made the most sacrifices,' Gukesh had stated after his victory. His mother praised Gukesh's sacrifice and focus in turn. She said Gukesh had worked very hard since his childhood. He had been a disciplined child who had immense powers of focus and had sacrificed so much for chess. Padmakumari said that they were all extremely happy for this victory. Chess can be a lonely and cold sport and monk-like personal discipline is essential to compete and succeed at the highest level. Having the total support of family members

Alireza Firouzja and D. Gukesh at the Candidates Tournament 2024

always helps the cause as chess, like every other sport, is full of ups and downs. But the sheer mental pressure it generates is supreme. Unlike sports such as cricket and football, there are no teammates to support you when it comes to the crunch situation and you have to perform alone. Gukesh's father Rajinikanth was characteristically honest and humble when he was questioned on how difficult it had been for the family to support Gukesh to fulfil this dream.

'Every parent will do the same,' he said. 'If you see that your child has talent in something, it is your duty to allow him or her to flourish. That's all we did.'

It's easy to see why Gukesh is so simple, down-to-earth and humble just by looking at his parents. But it was a slow train that crawled up the hill as the road wasn't easy. Gukesh's family faced a financial crisis between 2018 and 2020, when his father decided to abandon his medical practice. This was a crucial decision as Gukesh was just cutting his teeth at the biggest level of chess. It was tough as travel to Europe to play in the big chess tournaments was an expensive affair. But somehow the family managed to keep the boat afloat in tricky waters. The financial crisis was resolved when the pandemic struck the world and Gukesh's father resumed his medical practice.

Even when Gukesh is travelling abroad, he does not indulge in an extravagant lifestyle, recalling the hardships and struggles his family has had to go through because of him. The only indulgence for Gukesh is probably food, and a popular restaurant called Spisoh in Norway is one of his favourites. Gukesh mostly orders takeaways from here but has also visited this restaurant with his coach Grzegorz Gajewski. One of the owners of Spisoh has revealed that Gukesh's favourite dish is aatu erachi masala, a spicy lamb curry from Tamil Nadu that his restaurant cooks to perfection. Gukesh and his family often ordered this dish, famous for its aromatic roasted spices, when in Norway. In fact, the chefs at Spisoh became so used to this order that they instantly knew that the Indian chess grandmaster had ordered it as the dish was not so much in demand among the Norwegian customers. But now who knows? When everyone was celebrating Gukesh's historic win after the World Chess Championship, how could Gukesh's favourite restaurant be left far behind? Spisoh's official Instagram account dedicated a congratulatory post to Gukesh as they celebrated the triumph of the youngest-ever world champion. Gukesh would have probably preferred a year-long free supply of Aatu Erachi Masala on weekends, but that's another story!

The Indian Candidate

15

THE ALMA MATER

Chess is a game of infinite possibilities. The thrill lies in discovering them one move at a time.
– D. Gukesh

Gukesh's alma mater, the Velammal School, has played a pivotal role in shaping the course of his destiny and his eventual rise to the supremo of the sixty-four squares. As many as twenty-two out of the thirty-threegrandmasters from the Indian state of Tamil Nadu have come from Velammal School. If Tamil Nadu is considered the centre of chess in India, Velammal School is definitely the hotbed or the epicentre.

The owner of the Velammal School, M.V.M. Velmohan recalls his first sighting of Gukesh as a ten-year-old shy boy who had impressed the chess co-ordinator of his school with his moves on the chessboard. The chess co-ordinator named Velavan Subbiah reported to M.V.M. Velmohan that he believed that this little boy had the potential to emulate the feats of Viswanathan Anand on the global stage and insisted that the chess prodigy be assisted financially. It is so important to spot talent before it gets lost in a country with such a huge population.

When Gukesh was crowned world champion, Velmohan boarded the next available flight to Singapore as this was a moment that he did not want to miss at any cost. It was a special moment caught in time for both Velmohan and Gukesh when they were locked in a warm embrace, as the photographers clicked furiously to capture the moment. Apart from Gukesh's parents, D. Rajinikanth and D. Padmakumari, Velmohan has been the biggest pillar of strength and support for the eighteen-year-old chess prodigy. He has also been one of the biggest influencers to enhance the popularity and legacy of chess in Tamil Nadu. The fifty-year-old Velmohan runs a school that has churned out so many chess grandmasters. This is where the dreams of famous players like Gukesh, Pragg and R. Vaishali began and took shape after careful nurturing. But what is it that makes Velammal School so special? We must rewind to 2013 to understand this. The school has been at the top when it came to the implementation of the 'Seven to Seventeen Programme', which was launched by former chief minister J. Jayalalithaa after the conclusion of the famous 2013 World Chess Championship match between Viswanathan Anand and Magnus Carlsen, which was hosted by Chennai. Under the 'Seven to Seventeen Programme,' each school in Tamil Nadu was instructed to teach chess to its students. But Velammal School appeared to be the one which took this most seriously as they did not just teach it to its students, but introduced chess as part of their curriculum. Every academic year, about a thousand children enrol in this coaching programme at the school now. The results are naturally fruitful largely because of the passion for chess here as they conduct competitions all year round, chess events and tours both in India and abroad along with the special coaching programme which enhances the exposure for kids. Both Gukesh and Pragg have been part of the school team that won not one but three world school chess titles. It also helps that big names like D.V. Sundar, former secretary of the All India Chess Federation, and Manuel Aaron, India's first international master have been roped in as experts by Velammal School to teach and nurture the kids.

M.V.M. Velmohan realized that travel and exposure were part of the learning curve in chess. So he decided to sponsor the travel of the students for chess tours and events and also provided education, accommodation and food, completely free of cost. Free scholarships and hostel accommodation were provided for the students who were the best performers in these events and tournaments. This was also a strategy by Velammal School to make a mark and stand out from the various schools in Chennai by choosing sports like chess, badminton, swimming, athletics, basketball, skating and yoga. Velammal School is a classic example of the fact that sport in the country can only improve if the government and educational institutions contribute greatly to it.

Every year, Velammal School invites world-class athletes to its campus to engage in interactive sessions with their students. This exercise serves as an inspiration to the students who are motivated to raise the bar and gain useful knowledge from these interactions. The sports celebrities who have visited so far include big names in sport like Viswanathan Anand, Sachin Tendulkar, Kapil Dev, Virender Sehwag, P.V. Sindhu, P.T. Usha and Dwayne Bravo. In September 2024, India's new sports sensation, double-medallist at the Paris Olympics shooter Manu Bhaker came to the school campus to present sports scholarships worth over ₹2 crore. But very soon Velammal School won't need to invite any more celebrities to give their students a pep talk as its ex-students could play that role.

Velammal School organized a grand reception for world champion Gukesh Dommaraju in February 2025. And this was not the first time.

The new target that Velammal School has set for itself is ambitious but achievable, looking at the work it has done so far. It has produced three great chess players in Gukesh, Pragg and Vaishali, who were all part of the Indian team that won the Chess Olympiad in early 2024.

'We are already recognized as a factory for producing grandmasters and a powerhouse behind India's chess revolution,' Velmohan summed up his ambitious target. 'Our goal is to produce a minimum of 50 Grandmasters by 2030.'

The future certainly looks bright and exciting for Indian chess.

THE KINGMAKER: GRZEGORZ GAJEWSKI

Grzegorz Gajewski is conveniently and popularly known as Gaju in Indian chess circles. The Polish grandmaster became famous in India when he coached Indian grandmaster Gukesh Dommaraju to a famous victory in the World Championship against the much-fancied Chinese grandmaster Ding Liren.

But Gajewski has had a long association with Indian chess. He was the second of Grandmaster Viswanathan Anand during the 2014 World Championship and has served as his second for several tournaments after that.

The association with Vishy continued as Gajewski was part of Anand's academy to mentor some of the brightest young minds in Indian chess. Gaju has been training Gukesh for the past two years, and thanks to him, Gukesh has considerably improved his opening strategy. Gajewski is a renowned opening theoretician in chess and also invented the famous Gajewski gambit in the Ruy Lopez opening. The gambit move 10...d5!? was introduced by Grzegorz Gajewski during a tournament held in Pardubice, Czech Republic (now known as Czechia) in July 2007.

Grandmaster Gajewski is an established chess player in his own right, having won many major European tournaments like the Polish Championship in 2015. He also participated four times in the European Team Chess Championship in 2007, 2009, 2013, and 2015 to win the individual silver medal in the first year.

Gajewski and Gukesh, Gaju and Guki to each other, have developed a special bond in a short span of time. Their diverse backgrounds are one of the factors that make their partnership tick apart from a shared affinity for lawn tennis and squash.

Gaju is a self-confessed fan of Indian cuisine and the kadai chicken is his favourite. He probably celebrated with his favourite dish and a few Indian sweets after Gukesh beat Ding Liren. This victory was especially sweet for Gaju as he recalled the ghosts of the Tromsø Olympiad in 2014. The man who beat Grzegorz Gajewski then was none other than Ding Liren.

Bizarre Chess Facts

Although chess is considered a serious sport and chess players are equally grave, there have been some funny and some bizarre moments in the history of the game that will make you laugh out loud or shake your head in disbelief.

- Consider this. A chess tournament taking place in Cleveland, USA, in 1973, was rudely interrupted when the police raided it. The cops not only arrested the tournament director but also confiscated the chess sets on which the tournament games were being played. The charge? Gambling! The cash prizes that were supposed to be given to players were perceived to be gambling money and the chess sets were gambling devices according to the cops. Maybe they should make chess compulsory among officers of the US law enforcement.

- The world witnessed its first grandmaster fistfight in the early 1960s when two legends of chess named Bobby Fischer and Pal Benko decided to use their fists instead of their minds to check who was superior. Author Frank Brady has penned this infamous incident in Bobby Fischer's biography *Endgame*. According to the book, Benko strolled into Fischer's hotel room as he was working with his second, Grandmaster Arthur Bisguier, who was also Benko's second. There must have been a real shortage of seconds in the 1960s. Thankfully, that is not the case today. Fischer asked the Hungarian-American grandmaster to leave the room.

'You can't come in,' Fischer said to Benko.

'Yes, I can,' Benko replied. 'Bisguier is also my second.'

'Yes, I can, Bisguier is also my second,' Fischer mimicked Benko in his Hungarian accent.

'Are you making fun of me?' Benko asked the young grandmaster.

'Yes, I can, Bisguier is also my second,' Fischer mimicked Benko again in reply and ordered Benko to leave his room. It is not clear who threw the first punch, but the heated exchange of words soon escalated into fisticuffs, and Benko emerged as the winner of the fight. Bisguier acted as the second for both parties here as well. Later, Benko regretted his action in beating up Bobby Fischer, adding unapologetically, 'He was a sick man, even then.'

♟ We know that chess players can be superstitious sometimes. Some wear a certain type of suit or a lucky shirt and some knock on wood before beginning a game. But what Russian grandmaster Anatoly Karpov did was uniquely bizarre. During the 1978 World Championship match against Grandmaster Viktor Korchnoi, Karpov decided that he would not leave any stone unturned in his desire to win. So he went and hired a hypnotist to help him do so. Actually, a hypnotist named Dr Vladimir Zukhar was one of the observers from the Soviet camp and Anatoly Karpov won him over to his camp, perhaps luring him with money, promising him a bottle of vodka or making a deal to buy his stamp collection. We aren't aware of the exact nature of the deal, and all this is mere speculation. But the good doctor agreed, and what followed next was simply hypnotic. The only thing Dr Vladimir Zukhar did during the match was sit in the front row and simply stare at Viktor Korchnoi with his huge, bulging and scary eyes. The grandmaster was obviously distracted and complained that Zukhar was hypnotizing him. Not to be outdone, Karpov complained that Korchnoi's sunglasses were deflecting light on his eyes and distracting him. Soon the contest got to both the opponents as they not only stopped talking to each other but also stopped shaking hands. The contest had literally got out of hand. All draw offers were conveyed through the arbiter, and there were a total of twenty-one draws in the match. During round 7 against Karpov, Korchnoi was a bundle of nerves and started shouting that he would come down from the stage and poke Zukhar in the nose. The hypnotist was removed from the front row after that, but the damage had been inflicted. Karpov won the match 6–5, and his hypnotist had played a major role in his victory by unsettling Korchnoi.

♟ Karpov and Korchnoi were involved in another infamous scandal during the 1978 World Championship, which is known as Yogurt-gate. There was tension between Korchnoi and Karpov when the former made a bizarre claim that the yogurt that was given to Karpov was actually a secret code that was intended to feed him signals about the position. During the games, someone would deliver yogurt in different fruit flavours to Karpov, which Korchnoi said was to help Karpov cheat by carrying secret advice. However, this bizarre claim was taken seriously, and during the investigations of yogurt-gate, chess detectives discovered that the first flavour delivered to Karpov was raspberry. No one had a clue what it meant, so it was concluded that raspberry could not have had any serious implications on the game. Also, it was delivered early on in the game before a critical advantage had been gained by either player. But a decision was reached that from now onwards, only a single flavour of yogurt could be delivered and that too, at the same time during each game of the match. Not fair on yogurt lovers like Anatoly Karpov at all.

♟ If you thought chess players couldn't get any crazier, wait till you hear about the Toilet Engines scandal. In the match between Grandmasters Veselin Topalov and Vladimir Kramnik at the 2006 World Championship, Topalov accused Kramnik of cheating. He said that Kramnik was making more trips to the bathroom than usual. Topalov's team said that they had been counting the visits and Kramnik had gone to the loo more than fifty times. Although this report hasn't been officially confirmed. To avoid further problems, it was decided that the private bathrooms of the two players would be locked and any further visits would have to be made in a public shared space. Kramnik was visibly dismayed at this intrusion in his privacy and reacted rather strangely. He sat outside his former private bathroom in protest, demanding its reopening, prompting an 'I told you so' from Topalov. But the bathroom remained shut, and Kramnik forfeited the next game in angry retaliation. Maybe Kramnik was not cheating and was just well hydrated. But the truth shall remain a mystery.

♟ If you thought that cheating while pretending to take a leak is preposterous, consider the curious case of International Master Igors Rausis. In 2019, this prominent grandmaster was stripped off his title after he was caught in the act in the loo. Rausis was using a chess engine while he was in the loo during a tournament. Rausis had been under suspicion for cheating as he had risen quickly to almost 2700 Elo in quick time.

♟ We have saved the most bizarre for last. How did the No.2 chess player in America play from behind bars? How did an inmate who murdered his mother became the No. 2 chess player in the United States of America? Read on.

Claude Bloodgood was up to no good in life, as he was in and out of prison consistently. Finally, he was sent to prison for life after his mother testified against him in a previous case. Bloodgood was so upset at this betrayal that he ended his mother's life with a screwdriver. Once behind bars, Claude Bloodgood decided to pursue his passion for chess for lack of anything better to do in prison. Surprisingly, he was an experienced chess player and organizer when he wasn't doing shady things in life. Bloodgood started organizing chess tournaments in prison, and no one suspected what he had in mind. He naturally won all the games as all his opponents were novices. But here comes the twist in the tale. Bloodgood formed a bloody good scheme. As most, if not all, prisoners did not have a chess rating yet, he ensured that the rated prisoners would lose all their games to the unrated prisoners. This caused the unrated prisoners to have an unusually high initial rating as provisional ratings have a large k-factor. Then they would all lose to Bloodgood, who would reward them for every point earned by him. Soon Bloodgood reached a mind-boggling chess rating of 2789 because of this clever scheme and he was only rated slightly lower than American grandmaster Gata Kamsky. This sounds unbelievably bizarre as Bloodgood did all this while he was behind bars. But there is another twist to this bizarre chess tale. Bloodgood himself called up a friend and asked him to report the matter to the US Chess Federation as to how an inmate had made a complete fool out of them using this loophole in the rating system. Bloodgood was a chess lover despite his murderous moves and wanted this loophole to be corrected that had allowed him to get such a high rating using fraudulent ways. The US Chess Federation did so and removed Bloodgood from the rankings. They also ensured that such a thing never occurred in the future. Stranger things have happened in chess. Bloodgood was known for his odd gambits in chess and even authored a few books on them.

GUKESH DOMMARAJU: A TIMELINE

29 May 2006: Gukesh Dommaraju is born to a Telugu family in Chennai to parents Rajinikanth, a doctor, and Padmakumari, a microbiologist.

2013: Gukesh starts playing chess when he is seven years old. He begins by practising for one hour for three days a week.

August 2013: Gukesh becomes a rated player in chess at age seven.

2015: A nine-year-old Gukesh Dommaraju becomes a Candidate Master.

2015: Gukesh gets his first accolade at the Under-9 section of the Asian School Chess Championships.

March 2017: Gukesh gets the title of international master (IM) at the 34th Cappelle-la-Grande Open.

2018: Gukesh wins five gold medals at the 2018 Asian Youth Championships in the U-12 individual rapid and blitz, U-12 team rapid and blitz and U-12 individual classical formats.

January 2019: Gukesh Dommaraju becomes the second-youngest grandmaster in the history of chess when he was twelve years, seven months and seventeen days old. He is the third-youngest grandmaster of all time.

August 2022: Gukesh wins Individual Gold at the Chess Olympiad.

August 2022: Gukesh beats World No. 1 Magnus Carlsen in the round 9 of the Aimchess Rapid online tournament. He becomes the youngest player to beat Carlsen, aged sixteen years, four months and twenty days.

August 2023: Gukesh reaches the quarterfinals of the FIDE Chess World Cup, but loses to Magnus Carlsen.

August 2023: Gukesh becomes the youngest player to

achieve an Elo chess rating of 2750, going past fellow Indian, idol, mentor and five-time world champion Viswanathan Anand.

September 2023: Gukesh Dommaraju becomes India No. 1 in chess and ends Viswanathan's thirty-seven-year rule as the top-ranked Indian chess player.

December 2023: Gukesh qualifies for the prestigious Candidates Tournament.

April 2024: Gukesh wins the 2024 FIDE Candidates Tournament and becomes the youngest player ever to do so.

September 2024: Gukesh helps India clinch its first-ever Chess Olympiad Team Gold medal, teaming up with Arjun Erigaisi, Pentala Harikrishna, R. Praggnanandhaa and Vidit Gujrathi. Gukesh also wins his second individual gold medal in a row.

December 2024: Gukesh is crowned world chess champion in Singapore after defeating his Chinese opponent Ding Liren. He also becomes the youngest world champion in the history of chess and the second Indian to be crowned world champion after Viswanathan Anand.

President of India Smt. Droupadi Murmu confers Major Dhyan Chand Khel Ratna Award on Gukesh Dommaraju. He received the award in January 2025.